High Recommendati  ;

DOING
GOOD
better!

DOING
GOOD
better!

How to be an Effective
Board Member
of a Nonprofit Organization

EDGAR STOESZ and CHESTER RABER

Good Books

Intercourse, PA 17534 • 800/762-7171
www.goodbks.com

ACKNOWLEDGMENTS
We gratefully recognize the efforts of Phyllis Pellman Good for her editing,
which increased the book's readability.

Design by Dawn J. Ranck
Cover design by Cheryl Benner and Dawn J. Ranck

DOING GOOD BETTER
First published in 1994. (1-56148-099-1)
REVISED EDITION, 1997
Revised edition copyright © 1997 by Good Books
Intercourse, PA 17534
International Standard Book Number: 1-56148-224-2
Library of Congress Catalog Card Number: 94-7314

Library of Congress Cataloging-in-Publication Data
Stoesz, Edgar
    Doing good better! : how to be an effective board member of a nonprofit
organization / Edgar Stoesz and Chester Raber.
        p. c.m.
    Includes bibliographical reference.
    ISBN: 1-56148-224-2
    1. Nonprofit organization–Management. 2. Directors of corporations.
I. Raber, Chester. II. Title.
HD62.6.S76 1997
658'.048--dc20   94-7314
                                                                  CIP

This book is dedicated to
Gladys Stoesz
and
Gerry Raber

TABLE OF CONTENTS

EXHIBITS

INTRODUCTION

Nonprofit organizations are about doing good. The purpose of this book is to help them to do it better.

The response to our first edition (1994), and subsequent workshops we have conducted with a variety of boards, suggest that many directors are serious about increasing the effectiveness of their service. We have incorporated much that we have learned from this interaction into this revised edition of *Doing Good Better.* We remain focused on addressing nonprofit directors in practical and understandable ways.

Our society is increasingly relying on nonprofit organizations as the federal government redefines its role and as the population grows. Happily, contributions to nonprofits are also increasing, although not in proportion to the rising need and expectations.

We observe that the nonprofit sector is not consistently performing at optimum potential. With each lapse, public distrust and cynicism grows. The challenge all nonprofit directors face is to rise to the occasion. Improved performance must, we are convinced, begin in boardrooms everywhere.

Whether it is an artist, a surgeon, a teacher, or a carpenter, to see a master at work is an inspiration. The purpose of this revised edition of *Doing Good Better* is to inspire and to raise the skill level of thousands of directors as they serve to benefit millions.

–Edgar Stoesz and Chester Raber

1.

ORGANIZATIONS:
Why are they needed?

> *"People are setting themselves more and more goals that can be accomplished only through large expenditure of money and large scale organizational efforts . . . Such goals can be achieved only by harnessing vast resources of talent, money, and organizational strength. That is one of the reasons why we have moved, as every society must, toward larger and more complex patterns of organization."*
>
> –John W. Gardner

NONPROFIT ORGANIZATIONS play a much bigger role in society than is generally recognized. There are more than 1,140,000 nonprofit organizations in the United States alone. In his two volume history *Democracy in America,* Alex de Tocqueville, the noted French historian, calls the nonprofit sector the most "distinctive and critical feature of American life." This myriad of privately financed, self-governing nonprofit organizations perform a variety of needed services, including day-care centers, clinics, hospitals, educational institutions, civic action groups, museums, and symphonies. It compensates for what economists call government and market failures.

Nonprofits, sometimes referred to as the social sector, take their place alongside business, the private sector, and government, the public sector, to provide people with the goods and services they need. Like the three legs on a stool, all three sectors are necessary.

The business sector provides jobs. It supplies the goods and services needed by a growing population. It sees that an assortment of fresh fruit is available on the nation's fruit stands daily—a remarkable achievement.

The role of governments—local, state, and federal—is essential. One has only to look at nations with dysfunctional governments to appreciate this fact. Governments are expected to make public policy and supply infrastructure and a safe environment in which people can be productive.

The role of the nonprofit sector is less understood, but no less essential. In 1995 Americans contributed $143.9 billion to various charitable causes. Eighty-eight percent of that was given by individuals.

All three sectors exist in most nations, although the load is distributed somewhat differently in each country. In socialist countries the social welfare role is assumed largely by the government. Most European nations, for example, devote more than 30 percent of their gross national product to social welfare activities, while in the United States the corresponding figure is less than 20 percent. Lester M. Salamon in his helpful primer *America's Nonprofit Sector* states, "The level of nonprofit expenditures in welfare services outdistances the levels of both federal government and state and local government expenditures on these same services."

Nonprofits also benefit from substantial contributions of time and labor. It is estimated that more than 100 million Americans volunteer an average of four hours per week to various charitable organizations. This converts into an additional $52 billion worth of contributions.

The biggest source of nonprofit income, however, is not donations, but fees for services. This is particularly true of health care, education, and social services which, in 1989, had income of $343 billion. Fifty-one percent of that came from fees for services, 31% from government sources, and only 18% from private giving. Combined, America's nonprofit, public-benefit service organizations had operating expenditures in 1989 equivalent to 6% of the gross national product. Comparable data in other countries is not available, but it is presumed to be much lower. In the United Kingdom, for example, the figure is estimated to be 2.5 percent.

While strong, the service record of nonprofits and Non-Governmental Organizations (NGOs) is not perfect. *The Philadelphia Inquirer,* in the spring of 1993, ran a seven-part investigative series, charging that "the nation's nonprofit economy has become a huge virtually unregulated industry." It disclosed such abuses as high salaries, high fund raising costs, and lean accomplishments."

The fraud and conspiracy trial of former United Way of America executives sent reverberations through nonprofit boardrooms. The same was true of the New Era Philanthropy's fraudulent contribution-matching scheme, which embarrassed a blue ribbon list of nonprofits in 1995. It is apparent that nonprofits, too, are not outside the pale of temptation and wrongdoing.

One Model Does Not Fit All Sizes

Every organization is unique. Each has its own history and genetic mapping. At the same time, many organizations have much in common. Whether young or old, small or large, religious or secular, nonprofit or for profit, they have many parallels. They have similar needs. They belong to the same species, as it were. Organizations go through similar stages of development which help to define and shape them. (See Figure 1 on page 8.)

Organizations are founded for a purpose. They don't suddenly appear out of nowhere. Founders are unusual people. They see an opportunity or a problem that needs to be corrected. They rally people to the cause, and the circle expands. A new organization forms; a new center of energy is created.

FIGURE 1

Stages of an Organization

I. In the beginning there is a founder (X).

X

II. There are converts (x).

xxXxx

III. A Board is organized, complete with Board Committees (BC). Volunteers (V) come forward to help.

xxxXxxx
BC vvvvv BC

IV. More Board Committees are organized, more volunteers come forward, and now there are also a few employees (e).

xxxxXxxxx
BC vvvvvvv eeeee BC
BC vvvvvvv BC
vvvvvvv
vvvvvvv

V. A CEO is employed and charged with the responsibility of carrying out the mission in accordance with the policies prescribed by the Board.

xxxXxxx
BC   CEO   BC
BC   BC
vvvvvvv eeeee
vvvvvvv eeeee
vvvvvvv
vvvvvvv

Some organizations advance from Stage I to Stage V and beyond in a few years. Some get stalled. Some die. The needs of an organization and the role of a Board change according to the organization's stage of development.

ORGANIZATIONS: Why are they needed?

The emergence and sudden growth of Habitat For Humanity International is one such development. Clarence Jordan, a farmer/theologian, and Millard Fuller, a lawyer/entrepreneur, each developed a conviction that shacks are an abomination to God and an embarrassment to a community. They devised a simple, practical plan by which deserving families could own their own houses. Hours of sweat equity substituted for the down payment. The cost of the house, with no additions for profits or interest, was spread over 20 years, making home ownership possible for families who previously couldn't even allow themselves to dream about it.

The idea caught on. Soon other communities throughout the U.S. and in other countries wanted to do it, too. Each was encouraged to form an affiliate. At the time of Habitat's 20th anniversary in 1996, it had more than 1,250 affiliates, including at least one in every state of the Union. Additionally, there are 260 affiliates in more than 40 foreign countries. Collectively more than 50,000 families have realized the dream of home ownership through this one prolific idea, implemented through a dynamic organization.

Benjamin Franklin was one of the most innovative of our founding fathers. Before starting the first mutual insurance company in Philadelphia in 1750, he started a volunteer fire company, which became the model for literally thousands of volunteer companies across the land, continuing to this day.

Founders are activists. They are risk-takers. They are innovative, driven by a vision. They get an idea; then they enlist the participation of others. Founders occupy a special place in an organization's history.

As an organization matures, it needs to change. The founders are no longer able to do it all themselves. The volume of work is too great, and there is a demand for special skills. This is a critical stage in an organization. It either stalls, or new vision and energy come forward. Founders must let go and find new ways to direct the effort.

Organizations at this stage may choose to relieve their over-burdened volunteer force by *employing* someone, often part-time, initially. This move immediately introduces a new and subtly complicating element. Now in addition to *doing,* a board must delegate and direct.

As the size and competence of staff increases, board members commonly feel that they are losing control. They wonder if the original vision is being compromised. They long for the "good old days . . . when things were simple and everybody was happy." Frustration may replace excitement. Joy may disappear. Crisis may fill the air.

Sadly, many boards are unable to make the transition from being hands-on, in which they do it all, to directing the effort through others. Such organizations predictably drift and grasp until they either arrive at a new definition of themselves (a definition that is appropriate to their new station in life), or they disappear.

On the declining end of the continuum are organizations whose light has grown dim or even gone out. They have a bank of happy memories, but their future is uncertain. The numbers have gone down, and everything takes more effort. Sometimes directors grow lax or weary. Sometimes the purposes for which an organization was formed are coming to an end.

The American Leprosy Mission (ALM) is one such example. Founded 90 years ago to minister to victims of that dread disease, ALM has rendered stellar service. In the last 10 years a drug cure for leprosy has been found, but 500,000 to 600,000 new cases are still being diagnosed annually. Many persons who have been cured will be forced to live out their lives with crippled hands and feet, unless corrected surgically. Much work remains to be done, but raising money and recruiting staff to treat a disease that has been conquered theoretically is difficult. The ALM board is faced with difficult choices.

The point is that over time an organization's needs change. In the beginning, creativity and spontaneity abound. Growth and maturity, however, bring the need for new accountability and organizational mechanisms. The founders would certainly have resisted such structures early on, and, at that stage, that amount of framework would have been inappropriate, but now it is necessary.

To perform at its optimal level, an organization needs a system of governance which matches its current stage of existence. The tendency is to stay with the old too long, to prefer the risk of inertia to the risk of innovation. As Millard Fuller says, "Get it right, and it soars!"

Changes in the Environment

Not only do individual organizations need to adjust to changes brought on by their maturation, they need to take into account changes in the environment. Some significant shifts face all of us on the edge of the 21st century.

1. Just as women have made their way into the marketplace, so they are finding their way into boardrooms. This welcome development expands and diversifies the pool of persons available to serve.

2. Boards are being held to higher levels of legal accountability. The thought of being sued while doing good is an offense to many old-timers, but the threat is justified. A board that conscientiously discharges its responsibility has nothing to fear. It is not endangered by a process which penalizes less scrupulous organizations.

3. Competition for cash donations is fierce. But today's shorter work week, earlier retirement, and longer life expectancy make it easier for some persons to contribute time. Organizations may find it beneficial to take this double dynamic into account in their planning, remembering that people tend to contribute where they have good volunteer experiences.

4. Contributors who are more educated and professional demand a higher level of performance. They are impatient with sloth and amateurism. They will tend to support only causes that produce results consistently.

5. The public is increasingly suspicious, even cynical, of non-profits. These organizations must earn trust by performing consistently. Trust should never be taken for granted.

6. There is a continuing trend toward localization. People want to see things happen in their immediate communities. They prefer something regional in scope to something national. Nonprofit leaders do well to respond to local concerns, while not withdrawing from global responsibilities.

Organizations permit people to do collectively what they are unable to do individually. Strong societies are made up of strong people, served by an array of effective organizations. Organizations are, we are convinced, a part of God's ongoing work of creation.

2.

GOVERNANCE:
Distributing the task

> *"'It is not right!' his father-in-law exclaimed. 'You're going to wear yourself out, and, if you do, what will happen to the people? Moses, this burden is too heavy for you to handle all by yourself. Now listen, and let me give you a word of advice and let God bless you . . . Find some capable, godly, honest men who hate bribes and appoint them as judges, one for every 1000 people; he in turn will have ten judges under him, each in charge of a hundred; and under them . . . If you follow this advice, and if the Lord agrees, you will be able to endure the pressure, and there will be peace and harmony in the camp.'"*
>
> —Exodus 18:17-32

ORGANIZATIONS ARE KNOWN by what they do. When directors meet, they talk proudly about programs they sponsor. Program is important, but before there can be program, there must be much other organizational activity. Furthermore, governance is needed, for it is the soil which supports and nourishes program.

Before there is a formal organization there are concerned individuals who have identified something they want to accomplish or correct. It may be housing for low income families, a school, services to the visually handicapped, or ways to combat teenagers drinking. At first these individuals organize themselves very informally, with the same persons doing both the planning and decision-making (which we call governance) and program.

As organizations mature and grow, these two functions become increasingly distinct. The board concentrates on governance, while the administration concentrates on program, under the direction of a Chief Executive Officer. This distinction is described visually in Figure 2, Organizational Basics.

Boards make policy. They delegate its implementation. Boards define the ends (outcomes) to be achieved. They delegate responsibility for the means (activities). Boards decide what is to be done, leaving the administration to decide how. They resolve; the staff act. Directors think. They perform a head function. They may or may not use their hands.

The separation between governance and program is, however, not absolute. Directors may help with fund-raising activities, and staff should help the board with its governance work. The two functions are distinct, but coordinated. The German proverb says it well: One hand washes the other.

The board's first job is governance; it sets the stage for others to get involved. Energy permitting, directors may also participate in program, but they may not do that at the expense of their primary governance function. When working in program, directors must be under the direction of those to whom the function has been assigned. A board functions as a board only when it is in session.

While serving as Chairman of Habitat For Humanity, International, I (Edgar) participated in the Jimmy Carter Work Project, building 30 houses in one week on the Cheyenne River Sioux Indian reservation near Eagle Butt, South Dakota. I was assigned to house Number 12. The fact that I was chair of the board was irrelevant. I was not performing a board activity. The board was not in session. I worked under the direction of the forepersons, Rose and John Morgan. I was one member of a crew of 30 eager builders.

Directors may learn this distinction intellectually, but ordering

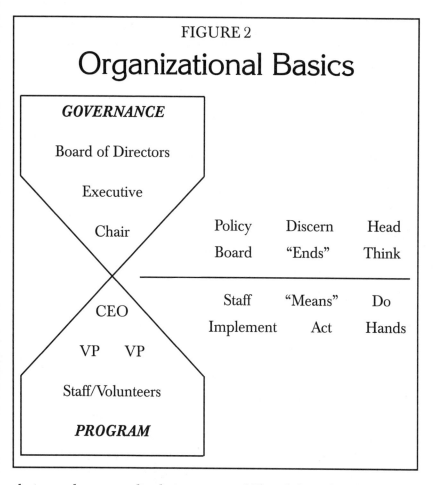

FIGURE 2

Organizational Basics

GOVERNANCE

Board of Directors

Executive

Chair

CEO

VP   VP

Staff/Volunteers

PROGRAM

| Policy Board | Discern "Ends" | Head Think |
| Staff Implement | "Means" Act | Do Hands |

their conduct accordingly is not easy. When left to do what comes naturally, directors are prone to do program at the expense of governance. Program has tangible rewards, while governance seems abstract. In young and in small organizations, directors tend to become involved in program. In fact, they may hesitate to release that role, even when their board function becomes heavier. This stunts the organization and leads to burnout.

The temptation for directors to concentrate on program when they should be doing the work of the board also results from another fact. In their regular employment, most directors serve in a staff capacity—

they are under-the-line, carrying out decisions made by others.

On occasion someone may move from serving as a director to a staff role, or vice versa. They cross over the line, calling for a new way of thinking.

Use of Board Committees

Committees may serve either a governance or a program function. Both are legitimate, although it is necessary to be clear about which is expected.

Many organizations, particularly small ones, rely on committees for program implementation. That can be useful; indeed, in some organizations it is necessary. But it can also be confusing if the governance and program roles are combined. Directors who serve in this dual capacity must learn to discipline themselves accordingly. They must above all remember that the committee of which they are a part has only the authority granted it by the board.

By subdividing into committees, a board may do its governance work more thoroughly. John Carver suggests that committees do pre- and post-board meeting work. That is, they prepare proposals for board action and guide implementation of previous actions.

Every committee's job description and its assigned tasks and goals should be written. Committees should be organized minimally with a chair and recorder. They are expected to report to the board regularly and present recommendations for board action. (See Chapter 8, "The Doctrine of Completed Staff Work.")

Committees, for all their usefulness, also have their downsides. Five problem areas should be noted, not to discourage the use of committees but to use them more effectively.

1. **Board Fragmentation.** A Board that is subdivided into functional committees, e.g., Finance, Personnel, etc., may become fragmented when, in fact, a board must function as an integrated, whole system. The recommendation of a program committee, for example, has immediate staffing and budgetary implications. The committee's work must be integrated into the whole-board work.

I (Edgar) serve on the Board of the American Leprosy Mission where I have been assigned to the development committee. Those of us on this committee have access to challenges and activities in the development area, but we get only indirect information about what is happening in the all-important program and finance areas.

2. **Dual authority.** Board committees have a tendency to pull the board's concentration below the line, getting it into the forbidden land of micro-management. The committee chair and the staff liaison must work together to identify agenda which is appropriate board work. An agenda drawn up by staff alone is predictably dominated by staff instead of board issues. Committee chairs must exercise extreme caution to avoid distracting from or conflicting with the CEO or the staff. A board cannot hold an executive accountable for results on the one hand and, on the other hand, authorize a parallel authority.

3. **Superficiality or redundancy.** A board that gives quick approval to the recommendations of a committee without probing the underlying issues is acting superficially. Quick approval pleases a committee, and it facilitates the meeting, but the key question is always, are good decisions being made? If, on the other extreme, a board insists on re-examining committee work in detail, that is redundant. Consistently finding the appropriate balance requires skill and discipline.

4. **Unintended and unforeseen consequences.** Some board committees, like the fabled British knight, mount their steed and madly ride off in all directions. They are perpetually on a "fishing expedition," to change the metaphor. In their enthusiasm they recommend starting this or stopping that without realizing that it may have unintended and unforeseen consequences for other parts of the organization. The result is that their actions often need to be reconsidered.

5. **Inefficient use of time.** Unless committees are well led, they use up a lot of time. They engage in more hashing than focused discussion. When board members are expected to serve on

numerous committees, in addition to attending meetings of the full board and filling special assignments, their time must be used efficiently and where it is of maximum value.

John Carver's surprising reply to the question, how many committees should an ideal board have, was "none." Carver suggests that a board should function as a whole and use committees only for special assignments. Only the board sees the whole picture. This is a corrective on boards' tendency to create committees to lighten their agendas, when they should be more disciplined about concentrating on governance issues and insisting on completed staff work.

The amount of time used in committee work can also be reduced by appointing smaller committees. Some committees need broad representation, but others function well with just two or three members. Some assignments can be done better by a single person.

Seeing how some boards function, one is almost led to conclude that committees can become an end in themselves, instead of a means to the end (the end being the identified mission).

Peter Drucker has observed that average organizations are distinguished from highly effective ones by the use they make of special task groups. Whereas standing committees are ongoing, a task group is assigned to study a specific issue. It arrives at its conclusion, makes its report and recommendation, and is dissolved.

Supervision

Governance has to do with delegating. Delegating involves supervision. She who delegates also supervises. Supervision includes a whole plethora of activities–planning, monitoring/evaluating, supporting, coaching/training, helping with career development, and promoting teamwork. Instead of a full discussion of supervision, we want simply to suggest a three-tier span of authority. Our illustration assumes an organization of at least medium size, although the principle can be adapted to smaller organizations.

FIGURE 3

Three Tier Span of Supervision

Board/Chair		
President, CEO	President, CEO	
Vice President(s)	Vice President(s)	Vice President(s)
	Department manager(s)	Department manager(s)
		Staff

The Chair has a supervisory relationship with the President. The President supervises the Vice President(s) and recommends their appointment to the Board, via the Chair. Similarly, the Vice President(s) supervise the department managers and recommend their appointment to the President. Department managers may be invited to make presentations to the board about areas in which they have special competence, but as Figure 3 illustrates, board members would not normally have official dealing below the vice presidential level.

In reality, administrative lines which appear so clear in theory do get compromised. A President bypasses, and thus undercuts, a Vice President when she deals directly with a department manager. A department manager registers a complaint about the President directly to the board Chair. This is not hypothetical; it happens. (Some practical suggestions related to these matters are offered in Chapter 13, "Conflict.")

Directors, like Moses of the Old Testament, sometimes burn themselves out because they do not give enough thought to how tasks are distributed. They forget that the best directors are not those who do the work of two, or even five, but who organize the work for 50!

Program is expected to do things right. Governance is responsible to do right things.

3.

DIRECTORS:
Their duties and responsibilities

> *"Board difficulties are not a problem of people, but of process. The problems lie squarely in our widely accepted approach to governance, including its treatment of board job design, board-staff relationships, the chief executive role, and virtually all aspects of the board-management partnership."*
> —John Carver, in *Boards That Make a Difference*

GOVERNANCE, we believe, is the first duty of a board. We present six duties a board must carry out in the fulfillment of its governance responsibilities. To be effective, a board must do all six consistently. It can and should invite staff to participate, but the responsibility for these activities rests with the board. They cannot be delegated.

When a board is clear about its role and performs it conscientiously, it sets an example for the whole organization. When a board is unclear about its function, it is very difficult for the rest of the organization to know its function. Leadership begins with the board.

1. **State the purpose for which the organization exists.**
Organizations belong to their members and exist for a purpose.
The first task of directors is to understand what that purpose is and
to state it in bold and compelling terms. This statement becomes
the North Star by which the organization orients itself.

Organizational purpose is often summarized in mission or
vision statements. Organizations need both mission and vision,
but the two concepts are not synonymous. Vision is what you want
to be–tomorrow. It is an imaginary leap into the future. It is the
fulfillment of Robert Browning's poignant lines, "Your reach
should exceed your grasp, or what's a heaven for." It is what
George Bernard Shaw says so memorably in "The Devil's
Disciple": " . . . some men see things as they are and say why. I
dream things as they never were and say why not."

Vision is a young American President, John F. Kennedy, looking up at the stars and saying, "We will put a man on the moon
and bring him back to earth in this decade."

Vision is Millard Fuller surveying a ghetto and saying, "Shacks
are not God's will. Let's rid the world of poverty housing."

Vision is Waldron Scott, then President of the American
Leprosy Mission, saying to a disbelieving board of directors in the
early 1980's, "The goal of ALM is to eliminate this dreaded disease from the face of the earth."

Vision is Robert Allen, Chairman of AT&T, presenting a bold
reorganization plan to his board in 1996 to better respond to the
rapidly expanding telecommunications field.

Vision is a dream. It is a reach. It can fly. Organizations need to
dream.

Mission is what an organization is committed to do–today! The
mission is to realize the dream, at least as much of it as possible.
To realize the vision of a man on the moon, President Kennedy
created the National Aeronautic and Space Administration
(NASA). To realize a world free of shacks, Habitat for Humanity
International spawned a network of almost 2,000 affiliates, collectively building 40 houses a day.

The Girl Scouts of America work actively at their mission: ". . . to help each girl reach her own highest potential."

The three "musts" for a successful mission, according to Peter F. Drucker, are:

Need. For a nonprofit, need is opportunity. The more compelling and urgent the need, the greater the opportunity. The Salvation Army has become one of Americas biggest and most respected charities by its ability to concentrate on "raw" need.

Competence. Nonprofits must limit themselves to their field of competence. They cannot be all things to all people. Experts outside their field of competence are amateurs, perhaps even dangerous amateurs!

Commitment. Everyone, including directors specifically, must be committed to the stated mission and spare no effort in the fulfillment of it. C.N. Hostetter, the beloved chairman of the Mennonite Central Committee, was fond of saying, "The only way anything ever runs itself is downhill."

If the first challenge is to capture the essence of an organization's purpose, the second is to communicate it in ways that penetrate the organization. Vision and mission statements need to go beyond files and wall plaques and publicity brochures. They are, as we stated earlier, the North Star around which the organization orients itself.

2. **Devise a plan of action.** Mission statements are little more than fine sounding phrases until they are put into operation through a planning process. We distinguish between long-ranged planning (3-5 years) and annual planning.

The first function of the long-ranged plan is to anticipate the future. Directors are not seers who predict the future, nor do they need to be. Directors just need to be alert to trends in process. Even what we think of as cataclysmic changes are preceded by hints of their coming. Effective directors are preoccupied with the future, with what is on the horizon. They anticipate and are ready to respond to new opportunities.

Long-ranged thinking permits—in fact, it forces—directors to think about activities which seem beyond their reach now, but which will one day be possible. Long-ranged plans reach toward the vision. They represent a stretch.

The long-ranged plan forms the context for the annual work plan, which states what the organization is committed to do in the fulfillment of its mission. It includes goals and measurable objectives which facilitate evaluation. The plan assigns a cost to each major program, permitting directors and administrators to judge the cost-effectiveness of a given activity.

Staff is expected to participate in the planning process; indeed, staff is commonly asked to draw up a proposed annual work plan. But the board is responsible to set the broad planning parameters (budget level, areas for program expansion or contraction, etc.), and the board is finally responsible for what does or does not happen. (For a fuller discussion of "Planning," see Chapter 12.)

3. **Delegate responsibility for implementation.** Implementation of a board's decisions is delegated either to a committee or staff. Committees should have a written job description which spells out what they are responsible to do, as well as any applicable constraint and reporting expectations. Committees, even when they are composed of board members, do not have the authority to make or change board policies; only the board can do that. They should recommend needed changes for board action.

Larger organizations employ an administrator, commonly called a Chief Executive Officer (CEO). This person is responsible to the board. She is, in fact, the only person responsible directly to the board. All other staff are responsible to her. Some say that the hiring of a CEO is the single most important decision a board makes. It is, therefore, also its most significant relationship. A board owes its CEO three things:

A job description which defines the position's responsibility, authority, and primary relationships. Is she, for example, responsible for fund raising, or only expected to help those who are? Is he authorized to hire and fire? When is he expected to consult? What is her relationship to committee chairs? What limitations are imposed on his authority and, even, personal conduct? It is also helpful for the board to state how the CEO will be evaluated.

An annual review. Is the CEO meeting the board's expectations? Are the agreed-upon goals being realized? What is the quality of relationships within the organization?

A review can be understood as returning to the starting pitch—like striking the key in which a song is written after an a cappella choir has sung. The review is usually done by the chair or a committee of the board, with a report to the whole board. The review should identify both accomplishments and areas for future growth. It should bring tensions and frustrations into the open and explore how they could be managed better. These should be reviewed again in a mid-year conference.

The review process should be a two-way conversation, with the CEO invited to suggest how the board could be more helpful and how it may be contributing unknowingly to staff frustration. The annual review should be summarized in a letter for future reference.

Support. There may be areas of disagreement between a board and its CEO—it would be unusual if there weren't—but the relationship must be one of trust and mutual support. A CEO cannot serve a board well that she does not respect. A board cannot allow a person it does not respect to be in that office. The CEO must either be supported or dismissed. A CEO who is exhausted and overwhelmed by program responsibilities should not additionally need to question the support of the board. The CEO and board must stand in a partner relationship, sharing both burdens and accomplishments.

The scope of the CEO's annual review should also include the personal dimension. Is the CEO maintaining a healthy balance between work, family, and personal life? Does she or he have family worries? Financial problems? Hobbies? Longer term career plans? Health considerations? A physical examination should be required every three years, and more frequently as age advances, with a report to the chair.

A board can express its support by acts of special thoughtfulness. They should not save it all for the gold watch at the retirement party. Nor is everything communicated by a periodic pay increase. Board members may sincerely inquire into how things are going, give an occasional pat on the back, send a letter after a board meeting, remember the CEO's family and work anniversaries and birthdays. All of these are appropriate. They cost little and are worth much.

One organization we know hired an administrator who appeared to be the answer to their prayers. He was young and energetic and, at the same time, had a distinguished record of service. In the interviewing process he reminded them that he was a program person, not a fund raiser. Coincidentally, giving dropped shortly after his hiring, causing an organizational crisis. Simultaneously the organization was confronted with questions about its mission.

When the Chairman attempted to speak with the administrator about board concerns, the administrator stated that he should answer directly to the board. A board retreat was organized to deal with the issues, but it ended in a stand-off. Neither the question of the administrator's role in fund raising, nor the definition of mission was resolved. Contributions continued to decline.

Finally a committee was appointed to evaluate the administrator's performance. It soon became clear that he had lost the confidence of both the staff and the board, and that he had to be terminated. Both the board and the administrator were at fault. The board had never conducted an annual performance appraisal which could have identified and worked with these problems before they became paramount. The resulting pain and disruption could have been avoided.

In a well run organization, everyone from the chair of the board to the entry-level clerical person knows for what they are responsible and to whom, and who is responsible to them. Such clarity helps each person to be more responsible, productive, and secure. It also enhances the health of the organization.

If the first step in delegating is to fix responsibility for implementation, the second is to provide the accompanying instructions commonly known as policies. Through the policies it adopts, a board can gain meaningful control and reduce its risk of getting lost in the details. Policies are based on past learnings. They are built on values and, at the same time, perpetuate them. A board exercises leadership through policies.

Boards like to think of themselves as making policy, but, in fact, most boards don't make nearly as many policies as they think they do. It is possible for a board to go through meeting after meeting without defining one written policy. Many policies that are recorded grew out of a given circumstance and no longer apply. Even current policies are seldom indexed in ways that permit them to be consulted in a timely manner. It is almost as though the organization and the policies it has adopted live in two different worlds.

First, we recommend that boards inventory their policies. Only then is it possible to see which ones are out-of-date and need to be discarded, which ones need to be revised, and where policy gaps exist.

Second, we urge boards to consciously do their work from a policy perspective. For example, a Habitat for Humanity affiliate board adopts family selection criteria, instead of reviewing individual families for home ownership. The board can then expeditiously approve those families which the Family Selection Committee has found to comply with the approved criteria, and which it recommends for approval, and can reserve its energy and wisdom for those needing special attention.

On an ongoing basis, boards should examine each agenda item to determine if it is already spoken to by an applicable policy, or if a new policy is needed. Instead of reacting to individual concerns and questions as they arise, a board should establish a policy which applies uniformly to all applicable situations. Instead of setting the salaries of individual employees, the board adopts a salary scale. Instead of deciding mileage reimbursements on an individual basis, the board adopts a standard rate per mile. Better yet, it adopts the maximum allowable by the IRS, making it automatically adjustable.

Through well considered policy-making, a board fashions its main functions into a coherent whole. The Mennonite Central Committee, the relief and service organization of the Mennonite church, for example, says its policy is to respond to disasters first with personnel and, if necessary, with money. Staff is told "we are not a check-writing organization." Policies like that both preserve a value, which is based on experience, and give clear, practical directives to staff.

4. **Safeguard the organization's assets and insure its ongoing viability.** In practical terms, this translates into supplying personnel and money. Although the personnel recruitment and fundraising functions may be assigned to staff, the board is ultimately responsible to insure that the necessary resources are available.

It is an axiom that programs are only as good as the people who staff them. The board can help to attract quality staff by dynamically defining the organization's purpose. Strong programs attract strong people. Only small fish bite on small bait! People are willing to invest themselves in urgent and deserving causes.

Organizations owe salary and benefits to their staff which permit them to maintain a reasonable standard of living (including provision for college education for children) and reasonable retirement benefits. Organizations that try to do good at the expense of their workers, and that always choose the cheapest option, bring disgrace on themselves. Generosity is rewarded, and so is stinginess. Employees should not need to worry if money will be available to meet the payroll. Executives should be able to implement approved program without constantly worrying if funds will be available.

Directors, however, should not mistakenly assume that everything revolves around money. Employee morale is directly affected by how they as staff are treated. Thoughtfulness, respect, and affirmation are very effective and cost-efficient organizational lubricants. Again, the board sets the tone by how it treats the CEO and how it interacts with staff.

Planning for succession is a frequently neglected area of board responsibility. It is a sobering fact that most organizations don't survive their founders. From a board perspective this amounts to providing for its own and its CEO's succession, and requiring the CEO to have a plan in place to provide senior staffing continuity.

The second major resource is money. The board adopts a policy requiring its staff to operate by accounting and fiscal procedures which comply with all applicable laws and standard accounting practices, to have all legal registrations and filings in order, and to have accounts payable and accounts receivable current. The board approves signatories on the checking account and approves investment guidelines. If loans are necessary, staff should know what is the clearly approved policy on procedures and levels of authorization. The status of loans should be reported regularly to the board.

To insure that this is happening (and presuming that directors are not typically professional money managers), the board should engage an independent auditor to review the organization's records and procedures. Audits, it should be noted, are ordered by the board, and the resulting report is addressed to the board. Board members should study such reports carefully and discuss any recommendations and reportable conditions in depth.

In summary, the board is responsible to see that finances are available to operate the program it has approved. Board members should support the organization's fund-raising efforts, under the direction of whomever is responsible. Some directors may call on prospective contributors or accompany staff assigned to this function. They should pass along the names of prospects and assist with thanking those who give. Finally, every board member ought to contribute financially in proportion to his/her means.

5. **Monitor and evaluate.** Having delegated implementation of the approved plan, a board is responsible to monitor (Were the plans implemented?) and to evaluate (Did the program have the

desired effect?). Boards who approve annual plans year after year without knowing if their effort makes any difference are derelict in their duties. Nonprofits notoriously make long reports, even boasting about inputs—how many worker days or tons of this or that—but they are too often vague on outputs—what difference did it make? The assumption seems to be that activities translate into results. They don't always!

A new director of a respected Bible translation ministry asked how many translations were started but, for whatever reason (health of the translator, political interference), were never completed? Research produced a number higher than either the board or staff had anticipated. They took corrective measures, and an area of vulnerability became an area of strength. It all happened because a director asked for an accounting.

Reporting is not something workers do after their official duties are completed, in order to meet some bureaucratic requirement. Honest, analytical reporting is an integral part of official duties. The board should request the information it needs to carry out its responsibilities, and staff is responsible to provide it in a timely manner. Reporting should be a reliable account of accomplishments and disappointments. It should be objective and based on the approved plans. Most boards do not need more information; they need the *right* information.

Important as internal information is, no board should rely on it exclusively. It is a human tendency to under-report failure and over-report success, to be too self-congratulatory. Board members should make it their business to see program for themselves. The Habitat board feels strongly that to be responsible for an international operation, the board needs to meet in a non-North American location at least once every three years. When directors show up on the field, they should not undercut the administration. Directors on a field visit should have their ears and eyes open and their antennae out, and they should speak supportingly.

A board may occasionally request an outside evaluation of a major program, even if no crisis is looming. Outside evaluators look at the program through different eyes. They yield new insights to old problems and dynamics. They can be a good investment.

The results of program evaluation should be fed back into the annual program planning process, thus completing the cycle.

6. **Provide accountability to the members.** Finally, directors should always remember that they serve a public trust. They are responsible to give an accounting of their stewardship to their members, much as for profit companies report to their stockholders. The form of that accounting is very different for a nonprofit which is community based, as compared with one that has an international base. Although it may be difficult to communicate with a diverse and remote membership, that should not distract a nonprofit board from recognizing its accountability. It must strive always to understand the values and expectations of its members and those to whom it owes a review of its work. A board has a moral obligation to do this. Directors are accountable to the members who own the effort.

Boards also have practical reasons for reporting to their members. The nonprofit's most fertile ground for fund raising is its list of current contributors and members. Efforts to skillfully cultivate the contributing constituency, and to establish an enduring partnership with it, yield good results. People who believe in the cause, who are supplied with reports that are informational and not overly self-serving, can be motivated to increase their giving. They tell their friends, and the circle of support expands.

Annual reporting should be provided in a form that is appropriate to the size and values of the membership. It should not be too voluminous or expensive, nor should it be too brief or non-professional. Members should be informed that an annual independent audit has been completed and that condensed reports are available. Taking a cue from the for profit world, nonprofit reports should be addressed to the membership.

Boards who perform these six activities skillfully and consistently are doing their job. Boards that do four of the six do not get a passing grade; all six are necessary.

4.

BOARDS:
How are they assembled and nurtured?

> *"Many are called, but few are chosen."*
>
> —Jesus, Matthew 22:14

WHERE CAN PEOPLE be found to perform valuable board service, and what are their characteristics? These questions are being asked by new organizations, seeking to assemble a strong board, and by established organizations, working to keep their boards strong.

People are known by the company they keep, so our parents told us, and so are organizations. Directors who are respected within the wider community confer respect on the organizations they represent. Jimmy and Rosalynn Carter bring respect—even awe—to Habitat for Humanity by their association. What adds significantly to the Carters' contribution is that it is genuine. They don't just show up for photo opportunities. They share the mission and its values; they contribute their sweat equity with the rest.

A board is only as capable as the combined talents and experience of its members, plus the synergism which results from their interaction. No director represents all the desired qualities in full measure. What one person lacks is supplemented by the strengths of another. Through positive interaction, the directors stimulate and complete each other, so that in a healthy institution, the whole is greater than the sum of its parts. Sadly, the opposite is also true; a board dynamic can be negative.

Traits of an Ideal Director.

What are traits of an ideal director? We suggest five.

1. **Compatibility.** Do the prospective directors live the values and the lifestyle your organization advocates? Have they proven themselves to be persons of genuine compassion and generous spirit? Are they already supporters of your organization or similar causes? Is their motive one of service and not self-interest? Have they been associated with activities which would reflect negatively on your organization?

2. **Judgment.** Can they sort through the maze of complex issues and arrive at a wise conclusion? We all know persons who are dedicated and knowledgeable, but who lack sound judgment. Judgment is that elusive quality which combines knowledge and experience, permitting a director to discern if something has merit or if it will prove to be an expensive distraction. Effective directors are capable of independent judgment, while at the same time they are open to being influenced and enriched by their fellow directors. A director who invariably agrees with the last person who spoke, or who always votes with the majority, is of little value.

3. **Justice.** Effective board members are persistent in their pursuit of what is just and right. Brian O'Connell in *The Board Member Book* calls it the single most important quality a director can possess. Knowing what is right is difficult, but a board is more likely to do what is right if it makes that its conscious objective. The tendency of many boards is to compromise, to look for an easy resolution. They attempt to contain a problem rather than get to the

bottom of it and solve it, and in the process usually exacerbate it. Directors who fear the consequences of doing what is right can anticipate worse consequences.

4. **Teamwork**. Board work is a collective process. The best boards are those whose members respect and trust each other. The best directors are those who, while exercising independent judgment, function also as team players. (That is a stretch but not necessarily a contradiction!) Board dynamics are delicate and can be easily upset by even one individual who, if not well led, can claim too much of the scarce airtime or act in an arrogant, inflexible manner. Lone rangers are not good directors.

5. **Doers.** Board service involves hard work. To talk about *sitting* on a board is an unfortunate misnomer. Board service is not meant to be an honorary position, although it is honorable. Through service on a board, persons of compassion use their talents and experience to enlarge deserving causes, while reaping deep inner satisfaction. Progressive and community minded employers increasingly free up their employees so that they can serve on nonprofit boards. Such employers view this as a good way to invest themselves, and it is, at the same time, good public relations for their company.

What about special expertise? Is the best board one on which a successful corporate executive serves as chair, the newspaper editor functions as secretary, the banker as treasurer, the pastor as chaplain, and the lawyer as parliamentarian? Not necessarily.

The ideal is synergism, not specialization. A board composed of one-interest people is a disaster. Well-rounded boards include people of divergent backgrounds, operating in an atmosphere where each one is complemented by the others. Individual members should have specialities, but board members must see themselves as involved with and representing the whole organization.

What about "inside" directors? Purists call for a clean separation between those with governance responsibilities and those with program duties. They believe that inviting a CEO to serve on the board clouds the distinction between above-the-line and below-the-line functions, and skews the agenda toward program rather than governance. Others argue that a CEO brings invaluable information, although that is available whether the CEO serves on the board or not. For profit corporations commonly elect employed executives to the board, but they are careful to insure a balance between inside and outside directors so as to safeguard against excessive self-interest, or the appearance of it.

We believe that a CEO can legitimately serve on the board in selected situations, if the respective roles are understood and adhered to by all parities. We also believe strongly that board membership should not be extended to staff persons other than the CEO.

Recruiting Directors

How can quality people be enlisted to serve on a nonprofit board? We believe that talented and dedicated men and women are available, and that they are, in fact, looking for deserving causes. Some are retired or approaching retirement, but many younger people are looking for another dimension to bring fulfillment to their active and successful careers. Women are increasingly making themselves available for board service; they are too often overlooked.

When assembling a strong board, avoid the wanna-bes and the has-beens, and look for the *not-yets*. Providing an environment where directors can grow and develop their skills is one of the rewards board members can give to each other and themselves. Boards should make people-development a conscious objective by offering strong in-service training experiences. Serving alongside highly successful individuals is a valuable education.

We suggest in Chapter 2 that an organization belongs to its members, and that a board is therefore accountable to the membership. That means one thing to an organization which is local in character and something very different to an organization whose membership may be national or international. It is virtually impossible to give a widely scattered membership the participation it deserves. Such boards become essentially self-perpetuating.

That is, the board, rather than the membership, chooses the directors. Such boards are in the vulnerable and ambiguous position of having fiduciary responsibilities without clearly defined and meaningful accountability.

We observe that individual stockholders are more able to participate in the election of directors in a stock company, through the proxy and accumulative voting provision, than are members of many nonprofits.

Directors must be persistent and conscientious in their efforts to stay tuned to their membership, no matter how close or scattered those members may be. They are responsible to provide as much accountability as the situation permits. Directors should seek to maximize the involvement of the membership, with a goal of forming an enduring partnership. They should look to members for discernment as well as support. Directors ought to make a serious effort to understand and fulfill the expectations of the members, in so far as they are known, and abide by their values. Directors who are unable or unwilling to do so should resign.

A geographically scattered organization can reduce such an inherent limitation by creating natural sub-groupings–regional, denominational, etc.–and invite them to nominate *representational* directors to the board. To be sure that the board has members who bring needed expertise and balance, these representational directors elect directors-at-large, so that the resulting board is of the desired composition and size. Representational directors are expected to report to the body that elects them. They are also expected to serve as a channel for special concerns from that sub-grouping, remembering, however, that all members of the board are expected to work in the best interests of the entire organization.

Some boards have the luxury of having more candidates than openings, while others need to engage in recruitment. Attracting strong board members begins with identifying a bold and lively cause, and presenting it enthusiastically. Ralph Waldo Emerson stated emphatically, "Nothing was ever accomplished without enthusiasm."

The call to board service must come from the right person, at the right time, and in the right way. Someone at the peak of her seasonal workload will predictably result in a rejection. Serious thought should be given to who does the asking, enlisting the chair for a particularly critical invitation. When the right person is asked in the right way, the reply is likely to be favorable.

Board Organization

Election of officers is usually handled within the board. To reduce the awkwardness associated with conducting a formal election in a small body, and to provide for this important function to have some deliberate and thoughtful process, nominating committees have come into wide usage. Called by such various names as Board Service Committee, Gift Discernment Committee, or, recently, the Governance Committee, the function has been expanded beyond recruitment and may include evaluating the performance of the board and individual board members, and providing for board members' training and orientation. The nomination slate commonly includes one name per office. Election is by acclaim. It takes just minutes of board time. There are no losers.

This appears to be a clear improvement over the open nomination system where everybody was eligible. Frequently little forethought was given, and it often happened that the incumbents were reelected in perpetuity, or so it seemed, not because of their superior qualifications, but for lack of alternatives. There were winners and losers, resulting sometimes in hard feelings.

Nominating committees, too, have their limitations. This all-important function is assigned to a small group. The possibility of nominating committee members seeking office for themselves or their friends, complete with political maneuverings, cannot be precluded. In a committee of three, a self-seeking individual needs only the support of one more person and a passive board to elect him-/herself.

The likelihood of a miscarriage of justice is materially reduced if there is open communication within the board, if the individual members practice independent judgment, if the board nomination process is thorough and close to the membership, if an agreed-upon board profile plan is used, and if clear election guidelines are drawn up. In a small board, defined somewhat arbitrarily as seven or fewer, the nominating function is better performed by the board functioning as a committee of the whole. The chair on that occasion should be assumed by a neutral party. The process should make it easy for the board to arrive at its wish without distraction.

We encourage larger boards, defined again arbitrarily as 15 or more directors, to consider electing nominating committees. They should be:

1. Elected by the board (not appointed by the chair) to avoid excessive influence by any one member.
2. Elected early in the year so its membership is known and so it has time to do its work well.
3. Elected for three-year terms, with staggered terms to ensure continuity.

Incumbents and persons thought to be natural candidates for an office are ineligible for service on the nominating committee, to exclude self-nomination. If there is a broadly supported desire to elect a member of the nominating committee to an office, that individual should resign from the nominating committee.

The importance of building and maintaining strong governing boards cannot be over-emphasized, since organizations seldom rise above those who direct them.

5.

LEADERSHIP:
Showing the way

> *"The mark of a leader, the attribute that puts him in a position to show the way for others, is that he is better than most to point the way."*
>
> —Robert Greenleaf, *The Servant Leader*
>
> *"If anyone would be first, he must be last and servant of all."*
>
> —Jesus

AN ORGANIZATION is a living organism which is constantly in a state of becoming. It is reaching out into the unknown to do what its supporters believe needs to be done. In a state of leaderlessness, it drifts and falls apart. To be effective, to survive in a competitive and rapidly changing world, organizations need to be led.

Effective leaders—not just nominal ones—cause people to want to follow. They do this by example, by the force of their personalities, and by selecting causes so compelling that people willingly sacrifice themselves for them.

Leadership should come from everywhere within a dynamic organization; it does not center only around the designated leader. Good leaders stimulate others to lead. DePree says, "The art of leadership lies in polishing and liberating and enabling those gifts [in others]."

Designated leaders are not always in the vanguard. An organization is fortunate to have pioneers in its ranks who are prepared to forge ahead. It is equally fortunate to be balanced by those who ask hard questions. Effective leaders draw the best from both and help the group to arrive at a decision.

The Content of Leadership

Leadership comes in many forms, even as leaders come in all sizes and shapes. The leader's style must be well matched to the needs of the organization. Robert Greenleaf has promoted servant leadership which seeks to fundamentally improve the caring quality of institutions through a new approach to leadership, structure, and decision-making. It is characterized by service to others, a holistic approach to work, and sharing power in decision-making. This is contrasted with a military style which can be appropriate and effective in crisis situations. Many leaders, servant or otherwise, use the charisma of their forceful personalities.

Personal style aside, John Kotter of the Harvard Business School, organizes the leadership task into three categories: visioning, aligning, and motivating.

Visioning

"Leaders need to have a sense of the unknowable and be able to see the unforeseeable," says Robert Greenleaf. They see the flower in the bud. They are on the cutting edge of tomorrow, pushing at the uncharted and the unknown. They are not content with the status quo.

Leaders are known for their creativity. Robert F. Kennedy enjoyed closing his campaign speeches by quoting George Bernard Shaw, "You see things, and you say 'Why?' But I dream things that never were, and I say 'Why not?'"

Many nonprofits, sadly, strive to give ever better administration to what amounts to second-rate ideas. They should heed Peter F.

Drucker who said that effectiveness does not come from solving problems but from exploiting opportunities.

Leaders are risk-takers. After all the research has been done, after the wisest consultants have been heard, there remains a gap of uncertainty which can be bridged only by intuition and faith.

Visioning, like creativity, happens only in a receptive environment. Alexander Solzhenitsyn, the famous Soviet dissident, in his 1978 Harvard commencement address said, "Whenever the tissue of life is woven of legalistic relationships, this creates an atmosphere of spiritual mediocrity that paralyzes men's noblest impulses."

One of the boldest displays of visionary leadership I (Edgar) have witnessed occurred in January 1992 when Millard Fuller, president of Habitat for Humanity, proposed a plan to eradicate poverty housing in Sumter County, Georgia, by the year 2000. At the time, Habitat had bank loans into the millions of dollars, resulting from a temporary and serious shortfall in giving. The feasibility study which should precede such an effort had not been done. Satisfactory answers were not available to such basic questions as, How many houses will that take? Where will the money come from? Won't affiliates in other parts of the country object?

The board was understandably and maybe rightfully reluctant, but Millard was insistent. The proposition was finally approved with some qualifications after hours of debate. When the news reached Sumter County, of which Americus is the capital, it was greeted in the local newspapers with the biggest headlines since the end of World War II. A bold action begat a bold response as white churches, who had never supported Habitat before, formed partnerships with black churches to build houses. A businessman donated a valuable 30-acre tract of land for building sites. Businesses made donations and the project qualified for grants. Eighteen months later even the skeptics had been swept along by the momentum of this cause. It was so bold that it was crazy, but it is happening, and other communities are being inspired by the Sumter example.

Aligning

Guiding an action from the idea stage to an approved resolution requires skill and, what is commonly known as, statesmanship. All action starts with an idea which, in the early stages, is relatively simple. In the process of development, simple ideas often become incredibly complex. Justice Oliver Wendell Holmes said, "I would not give a fig for the simplicity this side of complexity, but I would give my life for simplicity on the other side of complexity."

Before an idea can be supported it must be understood. The sponsors of an idea must be prepared to explain it patiently and repeatedly. They must be able to articulate why it is needed and what it will accomplish. One very good way to do this is through a written proposal (see Chapter 8, "The Doctrine of Completed Staff Work"). In the alignment process, obstacles are negotiated, fears are assuaged, and convictions are deepened. Everyone must be helped to develop commitment to the vision.

Motivating

The strongest motivating force is a compelling idea, well presented. Had Millard Fuller suggested that Habitat approve a watered-down version of what became the Sumter County Initiative, it would predictably have gotten a lukewarm response. Nonprofits need to continually coax themselves toward boldness.

It is dangerous to entrust a poignant idea to some people. They will either water it down to suit the most cautious constituent or make it so complex that people don't understand what they are being asked to support.

Early in my (Edgar) career, I worked for Orie O. Miller who was, in his day, probably the most dynamic leader in the Mennonite church. I noticed that when I left his office I was literally running. One day I said to myself, "Why are you running? A grown man, running down a public street?" Upon reflection I realized that Mr. Miller had so clarified the issue and made it seem so urgent that I could hardly wait to get back to the office to begin with its implementation.

The job market is prepared to pay the highest salaries for the gifts of leadership. Leaders rally the support of others. Leaders maximize opportunities. Effective organizations owe much to their leaders.

The Chair as Leader

Choosing a chairperson is an important decision. The chair must be well known and respected. She/he must understand the organization well and be dedicated to its mission. Her/his values must be consistent with those the board has identified for itself. Most of all she/he must be willing and able to make sufficient time available to serve in this capacity.

Some boards tend to elevate the person with the most seniority or prestige to the chair position. Being an effective chair has little to do with either. Above all, the chair is expected to facilitate a group process which draws the best from individual members and the collective group.

The chair and the CEO stand at the most critical nexus of an organization. The chair is responsible for how the *board* functions, while the CEO is responsible for the effectiveness of the *administration*. How they perform individually, as well as the quality of their interaction, set the tone for the organization. An active chair performs many functions. We will identify four major ones.

Access to Information

The chair is responsible to ensure that the board has the information it needs to fulfill its role. The old computer term—garbage in, garbage out (GIGO)—applies. The administration or board committees should deliver quality reports on the agreed upon schedule ungrudgingly. Conversely, staff has a right to expect that their report will be read thoughtfully and without fail.

For many boards the problem is not so much the quantity of information—directors often complain about how much they are expected to read—but the right kind of information. Information should be well organized. It should be concise and available in sufficient time to be read in advance.

Boards should have access to some information which does not come through the staff filter. One of the major reports to come directly to the board is the annual audited report. Board members should visit project sites occasionally, but, in so doing, they should concentrate on Ends issues and not allow themselves to get drawn into administrative detail.

A Supportive Relationship with the CEO

A CEO is expected to support staff, but who supports and who maintains a supportive/supervisory relationship with the CEO? The chair. It is one of his/her most important non-meeting responsibilities. The two should meet regularly, at least once between meetings of the board, to talk about issues they face in their respective assignments. They should plan together and dream together. The fact of just being together, like at a sporting event, may serve the important purpose of deepening their relationship.

It would be highly unusual if these two strong individuals did not disagree on occasion. They can and they should. But the disagreement must be at the objective level. It cannot be allowed to disintegrate and become personal or acrimonious. Should this happen, the board must step in and resolve the problem. Protracted conflict can be very detrimental to everyone involved and must not be tolerated.

Quite apart from their personal compatibility, the chair and the CEO must have respect for the *office* of the other. An effective chair does not usurp the authority which is vested in the office of CEO and does not denigrate it in any way. The effective CEO humbly and joyfully submits him-/herself to the board to which he/she is accountable through the chair. There is no tug of war and no playing of games. The atmosphere is one of mutual respect and collaboration.

Preparing the Agenda

Since the chair is responsible for how the board functions, the chair is responsible for the agenda. This is contrary to the practice of many nonprofits where the agenda is drawn up by the CEO, and the chair reads it for the first time as she/he draws breath to call the meeting to order. The agenda is a plan for how the board spends its meeting time. It should be drawn up weeks before the meeting by the chair in consultation with the CEO and distributed to all who are expected to participate, along with the necessary background materials.

Conducting Meetings

Chairing is more than ceremony and formality. The criteria for a successful meeting is more than starting and adjourning meetings on time and conducting them according to Robert's Rules of Order. The crucial questions are, Were good decisions made? Was the mission furthered?

Anyone who accepts the responsibility of the chair surrenders some private prerogatives. One of these is to enter into vigorous debate on all the issues. A chair who is not able to restrain him-/herself in this way adds frustration to the process which he/she is expected to facilitate. Because of these limitations, some directors believe they can have more influence on the outcome of a meeting if they hold positions other than the chair.

The chair is expected to allocate the available meeting time so as to cover the entire agenda. This is not an easy task in a context where freedom of speech prevails. It happens (not infrequently!) that boards strain at a gnat (often at the top of the agenda) and end up swallowing camels (often late in the meeting).

Important as the office of chair is, all leaders need to be reminded that they are servants, accountable to those who elect them. Greenleaf says it not once but twice: "No one, absolutely no one, is to be entrusted with the operational use of power without the close oversight of the fully functioning trustees. The enemy to effective leadership is strong natural servants who have the potential to lead but do not lead, or who choose to follow a non-servant."

Successful chairpersons are humbled by the responsibility which the office places on them. Lyndon B. Johnson, not one of the humblest of men, said it well, "The presidency has made every man who occupied it, no matter how small, bigger than he was— and no matter how big, not big enough for its demands."

6.

MEETINGS:
Gain or pain?

> "... *for your meetings do more harm than good.*"
> —The Apostle Paul to the Corinthian Church

WHEN TWO OR THREE people meet informally, they are likely to be rational, engaging, even charming. They enjoy each other's company as they freely exchange ideas on topics of mutual interest. Put those same two or three people into a meeting with six or eight others like them, and something changes. Some become shy. They clam up and hardly speak. Others get loud and domineering.

Boards are composed of different people. Some are right brain operators, while others are decidedly left brain. Some are cautious and examine every detail, while others enjoy the thrill of risk and adventure. The best boards are not composed of directors who all think alike. They are heterogeneous, but with a common commitment to the mission and with respect for each other.

Board meetings are a necessary part of organizational life. That is where a board does its work. A board functions as a board only when it is in session. It follows, therefore, that to be effective, a board must have productive meetings. That is the subject of this chapter.

I (Edgar) was having a meeting in Paraguay when a man walked by and asked, "What are they doing?" He was told that we were having a meeting. A puzzled look came over his face as he said incredulously, "Can't be—they are laughing!" Meetings in his mind were serious business!

We have all known staff persons who admit openly that board meetings are not their favorite activity. Some, in fact, find themselves with headaches, nervous stomachs, or other psychosomatic illnesses. This should not be so. If the board/administration partnership is what it should be, meetings should be productive and pleasant experiences.

There are many different types of meetings: all-day board meetings with a full agenda; special meetings which are called for a single purpose. A meeting may be for brainstorming, or it may be planned as a retreat.

Meetings take an enormous amount of time. A two-hour meeting of 20 people represents a full week of 40 hours. To be productive, meetings should include the following:

- A clearly defined purpose
- Role assignments: chair, recorder, perhaps a timekeeper
- Agreed upon time and schedule
- Agenda
- The transaction of business
- Clarification of future assignments
- Agreement on next meeting date, place, and agenda
- Evaluation

The success of a meeting depends more on the planning and preparation which precede it than it does on how the meeting is conducted. A poorly planned meeting cannot be conducted well. The key to successful meetings is planning.

Meeting Agenda

An agenda is a plan for the meeting. It states what will get attention, who will present it, and in what order. An agenda should be prepared by the chair and the CEO—it must serve them both. We find it is useful to think of meetings in three categories:

1. **Reports and resolutions** (The Past): This part of the meeting consists primarily of administrative resolutions, including approval of minutes, review and approval of the agenda and official board correspondence, and reporting. Reports permit directors to monitor progress on plans they have approved; they are important background for a meeting.

Before entertaining a new initiative, directors should know the state of the treasury and how the regular program is going.

Major reports should have been written and distributed and read in advance, making board time available for oral supplements and questions and answers.

2. **Business in process** (The Present): If in the previous section of the meeting we are concerned mostly with the *past* (reporting is by definition, *past),* we are dealing here with the *present.* This includes issues carried over from a previous meeting, and proposals having to do with programs underway.

Major presentations to the board should be in written form, concluded with a recommendation. Only items that have been properly processed and presented by either staff or committees should be placed on the agenda. Discussing a subject prematurely is not only a waste of time, it can be harmful. (For a fuller treatment of this issue see Chapter 8, "The Doctrine of Completed Staff Work.")

Many boards do not plan ahead adequately, forcing them to do much of their work in a pressured atmosphere. Too many decisions have short deadlines. Board members are too often confronted with less than desirable options, forcing them to muddle their way through. Muddling becomes a way of life for many boards.

Unforeseen situations will arise even in the best of organizations, and a board must be able to accommodate itself to them. Something is wrong when a board routinely operates reactively.

3. **Planning** (The Future): Planning has to do with the *future.* While not able to control the future, organizational leaders are responsible to anticipate it and to have a deliberate plan to make what is now a vision into reality. A full chapter–Chapter 12–is

devoted to the subject of planning. Here we only remind directors that time must be scheduled for this important board activity.

How to Use Meeting Time

When boards are left to do what comes naturally, they typically spend more than 50% of their time on housekeeping items. They use valued time to react to business that seems urgent, whether it has been properly processed or not, whether it is important or not, leaving little or no time for good planning. Boards get into bad habits and typically repeat this cycle meeting after meeting, year after year, while the organization winds down. There are many things boards cannot control, but a board can and must control how it uses its time

It is useful for a board to reflect on how it distributes its limited meeting time by completing the following exercise.

FIGURE 4

Distributing Meeting Time

Activity	Time presently spent	What should it be?
Reports (past)	%	%
Business in process (present)	%	%
Planning (future)	%	%
Total	100%	100%

Organizational renewal begins with the board, with how it works. When the board is clear on its role and does its work consistently and effectively, the rest of the organization follows its lead.

The Role of Debate and Dissent

Healthy organizations allow–even welcome–differing points of view. In a pluralistic society, it is said, where five people are present, there are six points of view. That need not be bad. Most ideas can benefit from processing. Few ideas, it seems, fall from heaven fully developed.

Ideas originate in creative minds, often in response to something which needs to be improved. They are refined in debate, and in this process they also become owned. Only ideas which can survive vigorous analysis deserve to be adopted.

A word of caution is, however, in order. Some organizational environments are so hostile to new ideas that they need protection. New ideas, like spring flowers, are tender and easily trampled. They must be thoughtfully presented.

There is room for an honest difference of opinion on many subjects, but our experience is that most prolonged and heated debate is the result of deficiencies in presentation and pre-meeting preparation. It should not be necessary to use board meeting time to refine a proposal and to clarify what was intended.

When the essential facts are on the table and there is a seriously divided opinion, the board has several options. If the issue is not urgent it can be tabled, allowing for study or rewriting. If meeting time permits, an effort can be made to arrive at a collaborative conclusion (see Chapter 13, "Conflict"). As a last resort, it is always possible to revert to a "majority rules" position. An organization must be able to arrive at a timely decision. Meeting times and energy are limited. The tendency to draw back from a difficult decision is ever present.

I (Edgar) was presiding over the Habitat board when there was heated and protracted debate over a recommendation to purchase and renovate an old building to serve as the corporate headquarters. The facts had been well presented and the board was seriously divided. At any given time there were three to five directors waiting their turn to speak. Suddenly it dawned on me that this could come down to the vote of the chair, as the body was evenly divided. I favored the resolution, but, had it come down to my vote, I would have voted against it on the principle that an action of this importance did not deserve to pass with a majority of one.

Dissent serves a purpose. Organizations should not run over it lightly or regard the dissenter as an enemy. Organizations need members who have the strength of their convictions. No one has said it better than St. Thomas Aquinas: "We love them both, those whose opinions we share and those whose opinions we reject. For both have labored in the search for truth and both have helped in the finding of it."

Meeting Ground Rules

Every board of directors must decide what rules will govern its meetings. Will the meetings be bound by Robert's Rules of Order? The rules produced by Major Robert more than 100 years ago are widely recognized as the standard by which meetings should be conducted. They have their value, to be sure, but they are, in the minds of some, more appropriate for the U.S. House of Representatives than for nonprofit board meetings.

Meetings must allow the group to deliberate in an orderly fashion and to carry through its will. The procedure by which this is accomplished should be appropriate to the size of the group and the wishes of the membership. A procedure which is unduly technical can be intimidating to persons who have not mastered Robert's Rules. Excessive legalism, too, can be a form of obstruction or manipulation on the part of a leader.

A Meeting Ethic

One of the bad habits boards fall into is to talk about people in their absence. I (Edgar) once participated in a meeting when the work of an absent member was referred to critically. A new member asked with an inflection of surprise, "Do we criticize someone in their absence?" In a soft but unapologetic voice he added, "I'd rather not."

We all had been addressed. Our new member had introduced

a meeting ethic which has made our communication more honest. No longer are people spoken about. They are spoken to, and that has both raised the ethical tone of our meetings and has made our communications more effective.

Brainstorming

Organizations must push themselves to get beyond housekeeping routines, to spend time thinking and dreaming about the future. A special retreat-type meeting may be called for this purpose, or time may be reserved in a regular meeting.

Brainstorming can be viewed as a mental walkabout. To be effective, the subject to be brainstormed should be carefully selected and clearly focused. Open-ended issues which are provocative and issues surrounding change are best. For example, how can we attract more young people into our program? Brainstorming should be guided by the following ground rules:

- The leader announces the subject and reminds everyone that all ideas are welcome. Nothing is irrelevant or impossible!
- Humor and wild ideas are encouraged. The leader's remarks should relax the usual inhibitions. The time limit usually can be short and should certainly not exceed one hour. No distinction is made between board and staff contributions.
- An understanding is reached on what is to be done with the results. The two obvious options are:
    - –interesting, but no further action is needed.
    - –assigned for further development.
- A recorder is appointed to list the ideas exactly as presented on a blackboard or flip chart. No attempts should be made to challenge or even to clarify them.
- Everybody is expected to contribute. There are no spectators. Contributions driven by passion are permissible.
- Long speeches are not permitted. Short soundbites are preferred.

The greatest value of a brainstorming session is that directors give themselves permission to think new, even daring, thoughts. It gets the organization's adrenaline flowing. Even as good photographers are willing to take 100 pictures to get five or 10 useful ones, so organizational leaders must be willing to sort through dozens of ideas before they find one that is deserving of their time.

Executive Sessions

While we advocate an open style of leadership, we recognize the need for confidentiality. Certain sensitive subjects should be discussed in a more restricted setting and should not include staff. Such matters are salary administration, employee credentials, performance appraisals, and disciplinary actions. Boards are encouraged to schedule sessions regularly where only directors, and others specifically invited, are present. The record of such sessions is usually kept in a different manner, depending on the confidentiality required.

Frequency of Meetings

A board needs to decide how frequently it wants to meet. The board of a young organization, whose members are local, may meet monthly, whereas the board of an older organization, whose members are scattered nationally or even internationally, may meet quarterly or semiannually. Large boards, whose members come from a wide geographical spread, may meet annually, but have an active Executive Committee in place.

Our preference is "not too often and not too long." A board that meets frequently predictably spends time on Means rather than Ends issues. It may be managing and not leading.

Long board meetings (for me [Edgar], anything after 10:00 p.m. is long) should not be necessary when the "doctrine of completed staff work" is adhered to (see Chapter 8) and when the meetings are well conducted.

Trees, we are told, die from the top down. The same is true of organizations. When a board is functioning well, as reflected in the quality of its meetings, chances are that the whole organization is functioning well. When an organization consistently has poor meetings, it is a sign of trouble. Meetings are a reflection of the organization. Good organizations have good meetings. Good meetings eventually result in good organizations.

7.

MINUTES:
More than a formality

> *"While the chair is guardian of what the board is* doing, *the secretary is guardian of what the board* has done."
>
> –John Carver

APPROVING THE MINUTES may become so perfunctory that it is easy to conclude that minutes are a meaningless formality. That is far from the truth. Minutes serve at least three important functions.

1. **Minutes are the official records of a meeting.** They record who was present, what was done (not only what was concluded), and actions taken by the board. Minutes record policies adopted and authorization given to do some thing in the name of the organization. Minutes must clarify who was authorized to do what, when, and within what constraints. If there are any related instructions, qualifications, or conditions, they should likewise be summarized in the minutes. A board action, in order to qualify as official, must be recorded in the minutes.

To fulfill their function, minutes must be specific and unambiguous. They must be comprehensible to someone who was not present, and to someone who reads them many years later.

Minute writing is made immeasurably easier when a meeting is conducted in an orderly manner, and when items for action are presented in written form. This permits all members to know what is intended, so that they can either approve, disapprove, or amend.

Before going on to another agenda item, the chair should ensure that there is agreement on what was concluded. Sorting out board ambiguity should not be left to the discretion of the meeting recorder.

Many of us have participated in a meeting where board members could not agree on a complex issue because it was not well presented. When an agreement seemed imminent someone said, "I move that."

"What?"

"What she just said."

"What was that?"

All eyes turn to the secretary who reads incomplete sentences from his notes. There is disagreement over what was decided, and the debate starts over again. Experiences like this try patience and thin the ranks of those willing to serve on boards.

All this can be avoided by insisting that, to qualify for board action, an idea must be thoroughly processed in advance and be available in written form. (See Chapter 8, "The Doctrine of Completed Staff Work.") When the meeting recorder sorts trivia from substance, the minute record may appear more orderly than the meeting itself.

2. **Minutes preserve organizational history and memory.** Minutes should be written with a view to history. When organizations celebrate their 50th or100th anniversary, where do they turn for information? To the minute book, of course, and their satisfaction depends on the ability of the recorders through the years.

When persons want to know why a certain action was taken, what the surrounding circumstances were, and what it was meant to accomplish, they should be able to find it in the minutes. To serve this function, minutes must record more than official actions; they should also include brief relevant background information.

The loss of an organization's memory is costly and unfortunate. It results in repeatedly reconstructing and reviewing what happened. Human memory is invaluable, but rarely can it be relied on for details. The written record is important.

In 1989 Habitat for Humanity passed what was thought to be a benchmark decision broadening the functions and prerogatives of its national program. Soon thereafter there were numerous staff and board member changes, and internal problems distracted the focus. In 1993 a completely different staff and committee spent many hours examining the same issues and arrived at very similar conclusions, without being aware of the earlier action. In the meanwhile, valuable time was lost. Sometimes organizations are like the Corn Flakes ad: "Eat them again for the first time."

3. **Minutes are an organization's legal records.** If your organization is sued—and organizations are being sued—the minute book is the first document the attorney will request. Minutes record who was present, what was on the agenda, and how the individual directors voted on a particular issue. This will help to determine if the directors individually, and the board collectively, practiced due diligence in the exercise of their responsibilities.

Minutes should be written with legal liability in mind. A director who votes against an action that is approved should ask that her vote be recorded in the minutes. The attorney's contention that a board did not comply with a reasonable standard of care can be refuted by a reference in the minutes to a discussion that took place on a certain date. An individual director may get himself removed from litigation by being able to demonstrate that he was absent or voted against a libelous action. A director who tries unsuccessfully to have the board establish a grievance procedure should insist that it be recorded in the minutes. When a director declines to participate in the discussion of an item on which he or she has a conflict of interest, that should be noted in the minutes.

Most bylaws assign responsibility for the minute record to the secretary. Some boards appoint a non-board member to assist in minute keeping, thus permitting the secretary more active participation in the meeting. This is acceptable as long as it is understood that the secretary is ultimately responsible for the record. Normally, someone responsible to implement board actions (usually staff) should not be asked to record the minutes.

Allowing the chair to approve the minutes is a good procedure practiced by many organizations.

The pages in the minute book should be numbered. All minutes should be signed by the secretary.

Minutes should be available in draft form within days after a meeting and should be distributed to the membership within a week of the meeting. The value of a meeting is diminished by a delay in getting the minutes out. When minutes have been distributed, it should not be necessary to read them at the next meeting, although organizations that meet infrequently may benefit from a review of the major actions. Minutes are official only after they have been approved by the board.

Recording a discussion-type meeting is both difficult and important. The value of a day's work can easily be lost by a careless or inept recorder. Inversely, a skillful recorder can add focus to a meeting without embellishing it. Recording machines and laptop word processors are increasingly making their way into boardrooms, and they can help to record what was said, although care should be taken not to put excessive detail into the minutes.

The body of minutes can be shortened and the authenticity of the record increased by making major presentations an attachment to the minutes. The manager's report or the financial report, for example, may be attached and, therefore, does not need to be summarized in detail. The secretary should specify which reports are attachments, and they should be an official part of the minute record.

Minutes should be catalogued by subject for easy reference.

Maintaining a good minute record is a necessary part of organizational management. The quality of an organization is apparent in the minutes. Ineffective organizations may have good minutes, but strong organizations rarely have poor minutes.

8.

THE DOCTRINE
of completed staff work

> *"No presente problemas, soluciones."*
> *(Don't present problems; solutions.)*
> —A Spanish proverb

ISSUES MUST BE well thought through and processed before they are presented to the board for action. "No raw meat," we say. "Everything must be pre-cooked."

It may sound simple, but it is not easy and is often violated. Inadequate meeting preparation probably contributes more to long and bungled meetings, poor decisions, and low director morale than any other single thing. This can be corrected, and board effectiveness and efficiency can be improved.

A weak or an inexperienced executive or committee chair may describe an idea or a problem to the board in a general way, ending with, What do you think? What should we do? He folds his hands into his lap and assumes that he has done his job. But instead of leading the board and facilitating the process, he has presented it with several problems.

To take a raw idea or problem and prepare it for board action in the form of a written proposal takes time and requires some effort and skill. This work must be done by staff or a committee before the meeting. The board should resolutely refuse to spend time on issues which have not been properly prepared in advance.

Proposal Development

Proposals are the link between an idea and action. They come in response to either a problem or an opportunity. Written proposals prepare an idea in such a manner that its merits can be evaluated. Leadership is expressed through proposals.

The seminal idea, which is the core of a proposal, can originate with any person at any time. Regardless of its origin, its merits must be carefully and respectfully evaluated. Some ideas, for a variety of valid reasons, never make the grade. Most ideas are substantially changed while they are developing. An idea under serious consideration should be expressed in the form of a written proposal so that it can be carefully evaluated. A well prepared proposal must include the following information:

1. **Who** is making the proposal?
2. **To whom** is it addressed?
3. **When** is it being made?
4. **What** is being proposed? (For example, it may be a plan to expand fund raising.)
5. **Why** is the proposed action needed? Identify the problem or the opportunity which is calling for the proposed action.
6. **What** will it accomplish? State the specific goals and relate them to the organization's mission.
7. **What** will it cost? Capital expenditures? Projected first-year operating cost? Projected five-year operating cost? (The cost should be related to the projected benefits.)
8. **Where** is this activity to take place?
9. **When** will it be implemented? When will it be evaluated? What is the intended duration of this activity?
10. **List several alternatives** which have been carefully considered and eliminated for whatever reason. Listing questions

remaining to be explored reveals the incompleteness of a proposal but may add comprehensiveness and credibility to a proposal.

Seldom should a proposal exceed one or two pages in length, although it can be supplemented by attachments.

A proposal is not ready for board action until it has been cleared by all who are directly implicated by it. Staff members or other board committees who are affected by a proposal should be consulted before it is presented to the board for action. For example, the financial implications of a proposal are related to the budget and should be discussed with the finance committee or department in advance. The same principle applies to staffing or other implications.

What if staff or the sponsoring board committee are not of one mind regarding the merits or content of a proposal? We believe that the proposal is then not yet ready for presentation. But, in the end, if not everyone can agree but the proposal has substantial support, it should be presented with a brief but fair reference to the dissenting points of view. The final decision belongs with the board. If the proposal is approved, everyone, supporters and dissenters alike, should work together to put it into action.

Board Options

A board is expected to examine new proposals vigorously. An idea which cannot survive critical examination does not deserve to be adopted. Having completed its review, a board of directors has one of three options:

1. **Approve:** Before a proposal is approved it belongs to the presenter(s). It has no official status. Once approved, it belongs to the organization who is responsible for it. The enabling minute should delegate responsibility for its implementation. Conditions attached to the approval should be stated clearly.

2. **Disapprove:** The board may feel that the proposal is not within the organization's mission, or that funding or staffing are

not available. Directors should not give their approval against their better judgment.

3. **Amend:** A board has the prerogative to scale a proposal up or down or to amend it in whatever way it chooses. It should, however, not allow itself to be drawn into a time-consuming exercise. If the amendments are major, the proposal should be tabled and rescheduled for the next meeting. Hasty approval often results in unnecessary problems and complications later.

A board is rightfully judged by the quality of its decisions. Good decisions are based on carefully gathered and presented information. Practicing the doctrine of completed staff (and committee) work increases organizational effectiveness. It raises morale and fosters a spirit of teamwork.

9.

MONEY:
It is necessary

> *"The ultimate questions, which I think people in the nonprofit organization should be asking again and again and again, both of themselves and of the institution, are: What should I hold myself accountable for by way of contributions and results? What should this institution hold itself accountable for by way of contributions and results? What should this institution and I be remembered for?"*
> —Peter F. Drucker

ULTIMATELY, IN OUR WORLD, many things we want have financial implications. A friend, who was the best treasurer an organization could wish to have, was fond of saying, "Money isn't everything, but it sure beats whatever is in second place." Spoken as a true treasurer? Perhaps, but try running an organization without money, or with too little money! It changes everything. Ultimately, in our world, things have a way of needing money.

Many nonprofit organizations are firm in their belief that their workers, the volunteers, are their most valued resource. But even volunteers cost money, and when there isn't enough of it, their number is reduced and their effectiveness is hindered. The important role money plays in the life of an organization cannot be denied.

There are, when you stop to think of it, four things organizations do with money:

1) They earn it through fees for services.
2) They raise it by inviting others to support their cause.
3) They spend it in the furtherance of their mission.
4) If some is left over temporarily, and it should be, they can store it for later use.

In truth, there is yet a fifth thing organizations do with money. They waste it. Their biggest waste is probably not in poor purchasing practices or in frivolity but in supporting undeserving causes, in tolerating inefficiency, and in losing opportunities.

Earning Money

Many organizations derive a significant portion of their operating budgets from fees for services. This includes hospitals, retirement homes, parochial schools, camps, and mutual insurance companies. Such organizations need to put a fair price on their services and be businesslike in their procedures.

Raising Money

If governments get their power from their ability to tax, non-profits get power from their ability to raise contributions. An organization can achieve its mission only if it has a sound financial base.

We have all known organizations who exaggerate their accomplishments. They are sometimes described as organizations with a six-foot whistle and a six-inch boiler.

It is true, at the same time, that many organizations do not know how to present their work in ways that attract the public support they need and deserve. They are a light under a bushel. Organizations which thrive have both an effective program and a compelling way of presenting it.

An increasingly skeptical public withholds its support when it is not convinced that an organization has made a serious commitment to quality and excellence. Before organizations mount fund-raising drives, they should ask themselves what they have to offer and whether they are presenting it in a convincing manner.

Board members should contribute to causes they direct. This is not to suggest that the biggest contributors should automatically be elected to the board, but directors are expected to contribute in proportion to their means.

An organization we know discovered that not all of its directors were making an annual contribution, and so the subject was discussed by the board. As a result, they adopted a clear statement which said that in the future all board members were expected to contribute annually. Not only did giving increase, but directors also became noticeably more enthusiastic and involved. The leadership example of the board strengthened the base for future fund-raising campaigns.

Directors are expected to help with fund raising. In small organizations directors frequently raise all or most of the necessary funds. When an organization reaches a certain size, staff is retained for this function, but directors should give their active support to the fund-raising effort.

Not only are directors responsible to ensure that sufficient funds are available, they are also responsible for how funds are raised in the name of the organization. An organization's public image is shaped in large measure by how it raises and spends its money.

The public is preoccupied with overhead costs and rightly so. Many nonprofits have not proven themselves to be deserving of the public trust. Yet all organizations have overhead. We would not support one which pretends not to have overhead. Nor should it be assumed that organizations which claim to have the lowest overhead are automatically the most efficient. An alert nonprofit board keeps its overhead ratio under constant review and keeps it below industry or association averages.

Spending Money

Organizations reveal their true character by how they spend their money. Those with integrity concentrate their resources on their mission. Most organizations plan this through the budgeting process which serves the following functions:

1. A budget is, first of all, an incontrovertible statement of the organization's priorities and mission. A mission statement, valuable as it is, is words. It may or may not reflect accurately what an organization does. Anybody wanting to know what an organization is doing should examine its budget.

2. A budget is a plan which projects anticipated income and expenses before the year begins. If income and expenses are not in balance, ways must be found to either increase income or reduce expenses, or both. Wise budget-planning minimizes the herky-jerky effect which results from the irregular availability of funds which is so disruptive to good performance.

3. Finally, budget approval is important as an authorization process. When a budget is approved, the items in it should be looked upon as authorized. This is why approving the annual budget is one of the most defining and "owning" actions that a board takes.

Individual organizations evolve their own budgeting format. As in so many other areas, a middle ground must be found between a format which is so detailed as to be cumbersome and one which is so brief as to be meaningless.

A common mistake organizations make is to commit all of their anticipated income early in the year, leaving no room for crises or opportunities which arise in the course of the year. Some correct this through approving a relatively large contingency fund for appropriation throughout the year.

Thinking in one-year blocks is another organizational error. Long-term programs should not be operated on a series of one-year plans. As when driving a car, it is a good practice for directors to concentrate not only on the immediate, but also to scan the horizon.

A clear policy should exist about how much latitude staff has to move money from one budget category to another without approval.

Before concluding this section on budgets, we recognize a corrective offered by John Carver in his book *Boards That Make a Difference*. Without diminishing the role of a good budget, Carver says, "The policies represented (in budgets) are buried so well in numbers that few boards get past the numbers to any rigorous debate about the underlying policies. If anything, the numbers seduce board members into a myriad of interesting but peripheral details." Repeatedly Carver asks, "What is it in the budget that you want to control?"

Storing Money (Balances)

Increasingly, organizations need to have balances or reserves to carry them across lean times. Income for most nonprofits seldom comes in a steady stream which neatly matches expenditures. Organizations must have ways of managing those peaks and valleys so that programs do not suffer from seasonal fluctuation.

Not only does income vary seasonally, some projects are over-subscribed, while others have less appeal. This was true, for example, in 1992 when Habitat for Humanity received more than $5 million in response to the devastation of Hurricane Andrew. Organizations must have procedures to hold balances which have been designated until good program is in place to use them. Donors have the right to expect that their designations will be respected.

Accountability

Directors have both a moral and a legal responsibility to live up to their public trust. Trust is one of an organization's most valuable assets. Financial accountability is therefore one of a board's most important and non-delegable tasks.

Most board decisions are based on reports which are prepared by the administration. The board is responsible to approve the reporting format and the schedule by which reports are to be supplied. The formats should be understandable by directors who are not professional accountants and should permit the directors to monitor in major categories the income and expenses for both the reporting period (frequently a month) and the year-to-date. Included should be comparisons to the monthly and year-to-date plans and the corresponding period of the previous year. The administration should comply with the agreed-upon reporting schedule without fail.

The board may additionally want to appoint a finance committee to be composed of directors who have expertise in this area, who will analyze activity in greater depth and lead the board in this area of its responsibility.

All organizations, regardless of size, should have an annual audit. Audits are always addressed to the board, not to the CEO, because financial accountability is finally board responsibility. A newly elected director should ask to see the latest audited report. Any recommendations, and surely "reportable conditions"(or misdeeds), should receive prompt and decisive attention.

Some small and very young nonprofits find it hard to justify the cost of a professional audit. Minimally, such an organization should invite a committee composed of persons with good financial reputations to review the records, verify bank balances, and render a written report of their findings.

Audits normally cover only the financial activity at the headquarters level. They do not reach down to the levels within the organization where much of the financial activity takes place. This calls for a system of *internal* audits. For example, the Mennonite Central Committee, a world relief organization, is audited at the headquarters level by a professional public accounting firm. It additionally assigns staff auditors to perform *field* audits. This procedure extends a system of formal accountability throughout the entire organization.

Financial oversight is a major board responsibility. Board members should review financial statements conscientiously, along with program activities, to make sure the organization is performing its mission and meeting its ongoing responsibilities.

Nonprofit directors should also be knowledgeable about purchasing Directors and Officers Liability Insurance, bonding, etc. These issues are discussed in more detail in Exhibit 9, "Legal Dimensions." Directors should also avail themselves of books and professional advice on such subjects.

"What Is the Bottom Line When There Is No 'Bottom Line'?"

This is a chapter title in Peter F. Drucker's book *Managing The Nonprofit Organization: Principles and Practices*. Drucker reminds us that "performance is the ultimate test of any institution." Then he points out that "nonprofit institutions tend not to give priority to performance or results." Nonprofits are tempted to make their case by expounding on their good intentions or through obligating donors by pleading poverty rather than by demonstrating results. The results in a nonprofit that really count, let us be reminded, are those that further the mission.

Corporations are commonly criticized for being excessively preoccupied with the bottom line. But the bottom line, coupled with the need to have a competitively priced product, gives corporations a focus and drives them to efficiency for which nonprofits do not have an equivalent. We say, reluctantly but in truth, that we have seen long-term nonprofit employees who do not know the value of a dollar.

The public is rightfully skeptical of do-gooders who end up accomplishing very little good. The board of Habitat for Humanity has a need to know how many houses are being built. The American Bible Society has a need to know how many Scriptures are being translated and distributed. The Girl Scouts of America has a need to know how many girls are participating in their program and if, in the long run, scouting makes a difference in their lives.

10.

INFORMATION:
The way to empowerment

> *"Information free from interest or prejudice, free from the vanity of the writer or the influence of the government, is as necessary to the human mind as pure air and water to the body."*
> —William Rees-Mogg, Editor, *London Times*

THE PUBLIC has an almost insatiable desire to know. *The New York Times* offers us "all the news that's fit to print." Our society functions on information. We have newspapers, magazines, and books galore. We have telephones, television, photocopiers, computers, and fax machines. We have weather reports, market reports, and the Internet. We want instantly any information that affects us.

We also have a right to know. Information affects us, whether it is a scandal in city hall, a bomb scare, or a threatening tornado. Information empowers.

We act on information available to us. For example, once the public was convinced that pollution was a serious global environmental problem, many of us adopted less wasteful lifestyles. Today recycling programs are broadly supported.

To function well, organizations need to dispense information.

Much information is a matter of public record. Organizations are rightfully expected to make annual financial statements available. Public appeals must include some disclosure.

Organizations which are generous in sharing non-confidential information earn the loyalty and support of their publics. Organizations which share information grudgingly call suspicion on themselves. Employees have a right and a need to be informed at a level beyond the public.

How an organization handles information says a lot about it. In a healthy organization, information flows freely and accurately to everyone who has a right to know. An unhealthy organization is composed of a network of cliques. Information flows selectively and gets embellished along the way. Gossip is the everyday word that describes this dynamic.

Organizations contribute to a gossip mentality by attempting to be too secretive. We say "attempting," because most systems leak, and, when basic facts aren't made available through legitimate channels, imaginations and speculation go to work. Rumor is, in most cases, worse than fact.

The best leaders are surprisingly open in their manner. Guarding information excessively hints of insecurity and arrogance.

Information Carries Responsibility with It

The question Senator Howard Baker asked repeatedly at the Watergate hearings was, "What did he (President Nixon) know and when did he know it?" Consumer warning labels and tornado alerts assume that people are responsible to act on information available to them.

Directors have both a need and a right to know. They can't and don't need to know everything, but there should be agreement with the administration about what information will be routinely available and an understanding that no information will be deliberately withheld from them. Dr. David Hubbard, President of Fuller Theological Seminary, says, "We have a policy to tell bad news at 110% and good news at 90% in order to compensate for the tendency to cheat." Once information is in the hands of directors, they are responsible to act on it. Information carries with it the responsibility to act.

It is more difficult for directors to decide what to do with unfavorable information they receive about their organization through nonofficial channels. They have an obvious responsibility to hear it. They can and should ask some follow-up questions to determine the veracity of the allegation. Preposterous information should obviously be dismissed, but what if it appears to be plausible? There are several things directors in this position should *not* do:

1. They should not take unofficial and unsubstantiated information at face value. They should not be quick to believe the worst. They should assume an "innocent until proven guilty" stance.
2. They should not launch into their own unauthorized investigation. If they do so, they may add credence to what may only be a rumor.
3. They most assuredly should not confront an accused individual. Doing so would be indiscreet and could inflict unnecessary hurt.
4. They should not ignore it and wish it would all go away. Even unsubstantiated information carries with it responsibility.

What should directors do? They should report promptly and accurately to the board chair what they have been told. Then they should draw back and talk to no one about it. The responsibility now rests with the chair. The chair may already know about it, and corrective action may be under way. They may decide together that the issue does not deserve further processing. The chair may wish to discuss the issue with the CEO. The directors may want to check back after some weeks, and if they are not satisfied with what has been done, they should not hesitate to bring it up again. In an extreme case, they might even insist on bringing it to the board in a closed session.

The Need for Confidentiality

Not everybody can know everything. Not everybody *needs* to know everything. Confidentiality is necessary at all levels within an organization. Some information is not for public consumption, at least not immediately. The residents of a nursing home, for example, have a right to expect that information pertaining to their personal health will not become street talk. Banks and insurance companies possess information that must be kept confidential. Ministers and executives are trusted with information that must not be passed on. Journalists have the legal right to protect the sources of their information. Much information, including employee references, is gathered with a promise of confidentiality.

Processing confidential information usually involves informing other people. The circle of knowing widens. The concern is how to do so responsibly. The decision to share sensitive information must pass a three-point test:

1. **Necessity:** Is there a *need* to know?
2. **Competence:** The informant must be convinced that the listener is competent to handle the information professionally and maturely.
3. **Altruism:** The informant must feel confident that the listener will not use the information for her or his personal benefit or revenge.

Lapses in confidentiality have both practical and legal implications. Broken confidences create ill will and break trust which is hard to rebuild.

Legal Responsibility

Board members need to be reminded that on some issues, legal responsibility overrides regular procedure, including confidentiality. A board member, for example, who has information to suggest that a staff member is engaging in child abuse is legally obligated to report it to the chair, and they should together consult with the CEO. If there is an attempt by others in the organization to circumvent legal responsibilities, the board member who first

73

learned of the problem is obligated to report it, regardless of the consequences.

Closed Sessions

A board has both a right and a need to meet in private with only board members present, and it should do so regularly, not only in crisis situations. Certain information must be guarded, and some organizational procedures are best conducted in a less public setting. This includes disciplinary action, salary issues, and board debate on sensitive and/or personal issues. Soliciting the opinions of directors before conducting an evaluation of the CEO's performance is best done in a closed session.

The whole tenor of a meeting changes when the doors close. Directors who were too timid to speak before, or who spoke in a very veiled way, suddenly come alive. The discussion may advance quickly from established facts to speculation. Unless some discipline is imposed, an executive session can deteriorate quickly into irresponsible gossip. Executive sessions are nevertheless necessary and can produce good results when three features are incorporated into the process:

1. **A resolute search for the truth.** Directors do well to remember the warning of U.N. Secretary General Dag Hammarskjöld that persons who judge on the basis of one-sided facts are by definition unjust. The pursuit of justice must include a willingness to hear both sides before forming an opinion. It is never easy to sort fact from fiction, but wise and just decisions cannot be based on speculation and unfounded accusations. If the facts available are not adequate to conclude a matter, the discussion should be tabled until more information can be gathered. Going beyond the facts is not only counterproductive, it is dangerous. Closing the doors is not a license for irresponsible behavior.

2. **Involve the person(s) implicated as much as possible**. Speaking *with* someone is always preferred to speaking *about*

them. Before closing the doors, a board would be wise to ask itself what it is shutting in and what it is shutting out. In one such situation where I (Edgar) was involved, the facts had long since been exhausted and the meeting continued mostly on hearsay and speculation. When the person who was the subject of the discussion was finally permitted to speak on his own behalf, everyone saw quickly how incomplete the information was and how unfair the accusations. The meeting had been largely unproductive.

3. **Determine that the issue is ready for a board airing.** If a grievance is involved, has it gone through the board-approved grievance procedure? If it is a very personal issue, sometimes a pre-meeting with a smaller group is more appropriate. Often a meeting takes place before the facts have been adequately gathered. When a meeting takes place before the facts have been gathered and the best alternatives identified, it is likely to inflict more pain than it will produce gain.

Once a conclusion has been reached, the person affected should be informed immediately and directly. Sometimes it is helpful to do this in the presence of all who participated in the decision. A board must be willing to own its decisions and face people who are negatively affected by them, regardless of how uncomfortable that may be. Boards, for all their power, sometimes act in a surprisingly cowardly fashion.

We have both been on both sides of the closed door. We know how easy it is to be paranoid when on the outside and how easy it is to feel smug when on the inside. We know the dangers but also the need for a board to meet regularly, though not necessarily at length, in private. Closed sessions are, we are convinced, necessary and can serve a useful purpose if properly conducted.

Managing information wisely is an important organizational function. Effective communication is a discipline in its own right. Beware of the organization that hides behind anonymity and revels in secrecy.

11.

CONSULTANTS:
Helping boards
help themselves

> *"In dealing with experts, we may fear showing our ignorance
> (even though we may be entitled to it). We may also be afraid to
> put ourselves somewhat at the expert's mercy. Moreover, an expert
> often uncovers more problems than he solves. He may force us to
> focus on issues that we were able to ignore before."*
> —Roger A. Bolde in *Muddling Through*

ORGANIZATIONS are occasionally confronted with problems
which leave them baffled. It may be something internal, such as
need for a reorganization brought on by growth or the retirement of
a key employee, or it may be due to the introduction of a new service or technology. In either case, an organization may be like a sail-
boat. The boat is beautiful, the rigging is fine, the view is excellent,
but the boat can't move, or it is moving very slowly. Staff and board
have tinkered but can't seem to find the combination which permits
the organization to benefit from the gentle breeze. Sometimes a relatively minor consultation can produce surprising results.

Some organizations use consultants even when there is no major problem. They find that the participation of an outside person provides perspective on their unique mission and opportunities.

Directors are sometimes reluctant to engage a consultant because they see the action as a sign of weakness, or they fear that the consultant may confront them with something unpleasant which they are trying to ignore. Once the urgency is great enough to push them beyond these discomforts, they may become skeptical. "How can someone, who doesn't know our business nearly as well as we, solve our problems? And what is more, consultants are expensive."

Are they? What is the value of helping an organization get over an obstacle or meet a new challenge? The cost/benefit ratio of using a well selected consultant can be very favorable.

I (Chet) was contacted by the chair of a board dissatisfied with the results of its organization. He found communication with the CEO to be difficult. Employees, as well, were expressing dissatisfaction with management.

Within a few sessions the board became able to address each of its concerns. The board initiated two meetings per month between the board chair and the CEO to discuss the ongoing work of the organization and board/CEO relationships. Policies for the organization were developed, including that of the relationship of the CEO to the board. An annual performance plan for the CEO with specific goals was instituted. And, critically, the principle was established that all decisions would come to either the board or management by way of proposals.

Changes of this nature do not occur overnight, but within a short time significant positive results had occurred. The relationship between the board and CEO, and between management and employees, was considerably improved. Long-term targets for change were set in place. All participants seemed well satisfied with the direction and the immediate results. They look forward to the longer-term results of a more organized, confident, and clearly run organization.

For Whom Does a Consultant Work?

Do consultants work for the board or the CEO? The answer is either or both. When the issues being examined are board issues–for example, board organization and structure, philosophy of management, or strategic planning–the consultant works directly with and for the board. If the subjects of concentration are management related, the consultant may work for the CEO.

When a consultant works directly with the board, it may be threatening to the CEO. A wise consultant will maintain good linkage with all persons needed to insure the success of a consultation.

Practical Steps in Engaging a Consultant

The effectiveness of a consultation can be materially enhanced by adhering to the following suggestions:

1. **Describing the assignment.** What is the consultant expected to do? Answering this question well is the most important and difficult part of the assignment. The assignment should be described in writing and negotiated with the consultant until expectations are clear. It is not uncommon for assignment descriptions to go through multiple drafts. Proceeding without such an understanding is like committing to a trip without agreeing on a destination.

2. **Selecting the consultant.** There are many good consultants, but a consultant can do a good job only if she or he is relevant to the need. An expert is expert only in her or his field of expertise. Before a consultant is engaged, it is advisable to review a list of the consultant's clients, present or past, and get references from two or three.

3. **Agreeing on charges and timetable.** When will the work begin and when will it be completed? What are the charges, and when is payment to be made?

4. **Meeting regularly.** Consultants work best when they are in regular communication with the persons for whom they are work-

ing. Regular interaction is required to keep the assignment focused and to exchange pertinent information. If a consultant is being engaged to do a one-day seminar, those responsible should ask to review the preparation in advance of the meeting. The contribution of a consultation is better when the client is part of the process.

5. **Preparing to act on the consultant's recommendations.** Consultants do not make decisions on behalf of their clients. At best they help them to see the available alternatives and potential consequences. A consultation is not complete until those who commissioned it have discussed the conclusions thoroughly and thoughtfully and made provision for their implementation.

At this point the board is again confronted with the hard decisions which called for the consultation in the first place. Now, hopefully, the board has information which make the decisions easier. Failure to properly process a consultant's recommendations renders the effort a waste of money and opportunity.

Consultants can be viewed as regular employees, with one exception. Their employment is temporary. Consultants perform best when they are integrated into the ongoing process, when they are able to get well acquainted with the people for whom and with whom they are working, when communication between consultant and client is open.

Good consultants do not call attention to themselves or try to take a lot of credit for their work. Their satisfaction comes in knowing that they had a part in solving a problem or in recognizing an opportunity. They do not overwhelm; they empower. The best consultants can be described by the Chinese proverb, "When their task is accomplished, their work is done, the people will remark: 'We have done it ourselves.'"

12.

___

PLANNING:
Inventing the future

> *"Planning should be reality-based and vision-driven."*
> —Richard Celeste, Ohio Governor 1983-1991,
> Habitat for Humanity International Board Member

THE BEST NONPROFIT LEADERS see planning as the key to success. Asked to state the essentials for effective organizational management, their reply is sure to include planning.

While supporting planning publicly, many leaders are skeptical privately. They may have participated in a state-of-the-art planning exercise, or they know someone who has, and they were left disappointed. Even when they intend to plan, nonprofit leaders are not always sure how to go about it. They are busy and, against the press of operations needing to be done now, put off planning.

Planning is not a panacea nor is it optional. Planning is, we agree, an essential part of organizational management. There is good planning and bad planning, but not planning is not an option for a nonprofit that wants to be around in the twenty-first century. The future, we are convinced, belongs to those who plan for it.

What Do We Mean by Planning?

Planning not only helps us to anticipate the future, it permits us, within limits, to create our future. In the absence of planning we are the victims of our fate. We take what we get. We are totally in a reactive mode. Through planning we can be proactive. We can have influence, not total control, over the events which come into our lives.

A plan is a framework for collective effort. It permits everyone in an organization to see his/her contribution in the context of the whole. A single musician can play by ear, but an orchestra needs music.

By planning we simulate the potential consequences of a given activity, both negative and positive. By planning we anticipate the likely outcome of an action, permitting adjustments which lessen the negative consequences and accentuate the positive consequences. Good planning is one of the most cost-effective activities an organization can undertake.

Planning is not making tomorrow's decisions today. The purpose of planning is not to decide what should be done in the future but to decide what should be done now to make desired things happen in an uncertain future.

A plan is by its very nature static. It is frozen in time. It cannot be otherwise. Planning is, by way of contrast, dynamic. It is an action verb. It lives. It reaches out and thrusts itself ever onward. This is what caused an experienced nonprofit leader to say, "The plan is nothing–but planning is everything."

Who Plans?

To whom is this important function assigned? Repeatedly organizations have attempted to make planning a discipline which stands on its own, to assign it to a special unit or a consultant, always with disappointing results. Planning is effective only when it is an integrated part of management. Planning apart from management leads to what is known as SPOTS (Strategic Plans On Top Shelf). Management devoid of planning leads to irrelevance.

Planning is a part of every job description. The main difference is that the planning horizon gets shorter while the detail grows greater as the action moves down the organizational pyramid. For entry level workers, planning may have to do with hours or days. Board and executive planning is, by way of contrast, concerned with years and even decades. It is comparably "broad brush." In one form or another, however, everyone plans, and the nature of those plans must be appropriate to the position each person occupies in the organization.

The board is responsible to assure that planning occurs and to establish the parameters within which planning takes place. Perhaps most important of all, the board demonstrates by word and deed that planning is an integral part of leading and managing an effective organization. Management is authorized to act strategically and is held accountable for doing so.

How to Plan

The planning format must be appropriate to the organization to which it belongs. Many boards and staffs have been disappointed in their planning efforts because they used borrowed or inappropriate models. A one-size-fits-all mentality leads to disappointing results.

Unfortunately, the field of nonprofit planning is not well developed. Many books on nonprofit organizations do not even include planning in their indexes. Consequently, many nonprofits borrow their planning methods from the corporate world and may feel like David in Goliath's armor.

Our suggested planning outline is summarized in the Generic Planning Model (see Figure 5). It views planning from a *board* perspective since that is the focus of this book. It assumes a Stage V organization, so that organizations which are not at that stage need to make adaptations accordingly.

The Plan to Plan: The first step in a formal planning process is for the board to draw up a "plan to plan." In so doing, the board is accepting responsibility for the process. Through planning, a

FIGURE 5

Generic Planning Model (from a board perspective)

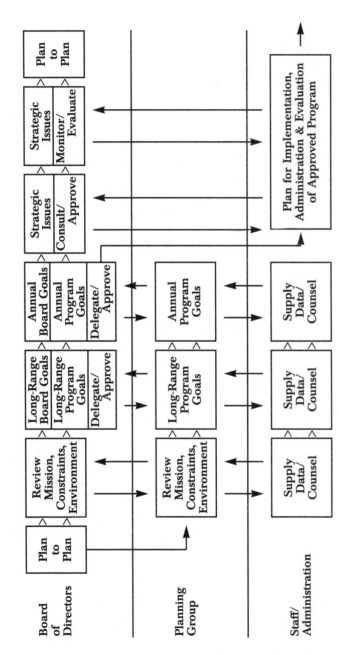

board is being proactive; it is leading. Boards that do not take an active role in the planning process are placed into a reactive mode. A board can and must delegate some planning functions to the administration, but the responsibility for initiating a strategic organizational plan resides with the board. The process begins with answering the following questions:

1. **To whom is the task of designing the plan assigned?** We suggest a committee of from three to seven members, depending on the size and complexity of the organization. It may include both board and staff. All those who are expected to participate in the plan should be represented on the committee. Persons who are well acquainted with the organization's history and persons who are known to be innovators should be included.

2. **What is the committee to do?** The assignment should be in written form and should state the expected end result. If the assignment has limitations, they should be stated in the memo of assignment.

3. **What documents and information does the committee need to complete its assignment?** This should include major reports, annual program plans and budgets, a statement of organizational purpose, mission, and vision. Most of all, it should include the last strategic planning report.

4. **How should the committee organize itself?** The board normally asks the CEO to serve as the committee chair. Additionally, the committee may have a secretary or recorder. In a large organization it is wise to assign a staff person to help with calling meetings, gathering materials, distributing reports, etc.

5. **When is the committee expected to render its final report, and are there predetermined checkpoints in the process?** Specific dates should be agreed upon and recorded in memo form.

Planning Foundations: The planning process begins with a "situation audit" which identifies the elements, both internal and external, which will impact the plan. Some of these elements are predetermined and cannot be altered, but should still be recognized. Other elements need to be challenged critically and updated. We suggest three categories of planning foundations:

1. **Purpose/Mission/Vision.** The focus of planning is on the Ends an organization wants to achieve. Have the purpose, mission, and vision been stated with sufficient clarity? The three are similar in meaning, but they should not be thought of as synonymous.

Purpose states the organization's reason for existence. It states the anticipated *results*.

Mission defines the *method* which will be used in carrying out the organization's purpose. It answers the questions organizational leaders should be asking continually: "What is your business? What *should* it be?"

Vision describes an organization's preferred *future* state. What do its leaders want it to *become?* For what do they want it to be remembered?

In all three areas it is important to remember the universal rule of planning–no organization will ever be greater than the vision that drives it.

The drafters of purpose/mission/vision statements should work for brevity. A paragraph of eight or 10 lines is ideal for a public statement. It is good to have a more detailed statement for internal board use, in order to elaborate on the philosophy which undergirds the public statement. One highly successful organization we know states its mission on a credit-card-sized card and gives one to each employee. If the employee can produce the card when asked to do so by the president in a chance meeting, she/he is rewarded with a five dollar bill.

The purpose/mission/vision statement is the single most important statement a board adopts because it defines why the organization exists. It is the heart from which everything else emanates. In navigational terms, it is the North Star.

2. **Constraints/Assumptions.** Constraints may be self-

imposed; for example, "Our business is day care." Constraints may also be imposed by the legal charter. Legal constraints should be recognized even if they cannot be altered, but self-imposed constraints can and should be challenged; for example, why do we limit our activities to day care or to certain prescribed geographical areas or types of service?

Assumptions help to establish the parameters for planning. It is useful, even necessary, to state explicitly what the planners assume about the availability of funds and staff or the anticipated effect of pending legislation. Sound plans are created from correct assumptions. When plans are based on incorrect assumptions, they cannot be other than faulty. And when the assumptions change on which a plan is based, the plans must be adjusted accordingly.

The experience of hoteliers in the early 1950s illustrates the importance of correct assumptions. They had every reason to assume that the logical place for new facilities was in the downtown districts. That is where the action was. Only by scanning the horizon were they able to see the coming of air travel and the Federal Highways Act which would keep traffic on cities' outskirts. The prevailing assumptions were wrong, leading to costly errors from which some were unable to recover.

3. **Reading the environment.** It is useful in planning to distinguish between the internal and the external environments.

Internal: What do we do well? What are our strengths and weaknesses? Our vulnerabilities? It is useful to identify an organization's core activities and evaluate their future viability. What is the average age of your work force? Of your key people? Are you state-of-the-art or is technology passing you by? Is your facility adequate? Are your employees being trained?

Careful attention should be given to what is happening on the periphery. What are the new opportunities that are waiting for their turn under the sun? Organizational leaders should remember that the Swiss had their first turn at the revolutionary digital watch, but they turned it down because of their single-minded commitment to the conventional watch (another illustration of faulty assumptions).

External: What opportunities and threats face us? One of the most limiting traits of an organizational leader is to assume the future will be like the past. It will not be! We do not see change coming if we are not looking for it.

What economic, political, sociological, or technological changes are on the horizon? What is our competition doing? Very few changes make their appearances out of nowhere. The precursors are there, but we choose to ignore them until the urgency is great. Then it is often too late. In this fast paced world, an activity or a technology which has been in place for 10 years is suspect. It may still have some useful life remaining, but it should be evaluated regularly and critically.

The board is responsible to lay the planning foundation by carefully probing and analyzing what is happening in these three areas. In our Planning Model, the planning group begins by reviewing what the board has concluded in these critical areas. In this process the board and the planning group should be interacting with each other, because the end result is foundational and must be owned by both groups.

From Board to Program Planning

This is the stage at which the planning process is divided into two parts. Having laid the foundation, the board delegates program planning to the planning group, while it concentrates on its board governance planning. The board agrees to a calendar of activities. It identifies the major issues it wants to address. It decides what committees will be needed and defines their duties and responsibilities. It decides how often it wants to meet and when and where. It identifies its future membership needs. And it remembers to monitor and evaluate the program it approved the preceding year.

The planning group identifies both long-range and annual program goals. Long-range goals, generally thought of as being from three to five years in length, are not intended to be operational.

Their main function is to establish the context for annual planning which is operational. Annual planning apart from the longer view often ends up being too shortsighted.

Long-range plans are more general than annual goals. Attempts to project five-year goals which are as specific and detailed as annual plans are not only counterproductive, they are frustrating. A development organization, for example, may identify continents and countries for future concentration. The naming of specific villages is best left for the annual plan.

Drawing from the purpose/mission/vision statement which defines what will be done, the long-range planning process focuses more on where, how, and how much. It seeks to identify what resources will be required and suggests what needs to be done to insure their availability.

A very useful line of long-range planning inquiry is what activities or services should be increased or decreased? Which should be introduced and which should be phased out?

The process of setting goals involves establishing priorities. Since resources are finite and organizations can't do everything, the process of goal-setting also determines what an organization will not do. This is difficult, and it is often painful, but it is necessary. Peter Drucker says it forcefully: "You must think through priorities. That's easy to say, but to act on it is very hard because doing so always involves abandoning things that look attractive, or giving up programs that people both inside and outside the organization are strongly encouraging. But if you don't concentrate your institution's resources, you are not going to get results. This may be the ultimate test of leadership: the ability to think through the priority decision and to make it stick."

Once the broad outlines have been identified, it is useful to set some specific targets so that all elements in the program can be adjusted accordingly. The addition of 50 hospital beds, for example, has serious and immediate implications for the physical plant, staffing, and cash flow. At this stage, the process does not need to go into architectural detail; indeed it should not. But identifying the broad goal permits the whole organization to anticipate and adjust its planning accordingly.

Establishing the correct target is both important and difficult. The electric utility industry in the 1980s seriously overestimated the nation's power needs, with the result that it finds itself with much under-utilized capacity. Underestimation can have equally unfortunate consequences. Computer models can help with this kind of projection, but finally these decisions are based on human judgment.

The planning group is expected to recommend its completed work to the board for adoption. Before the board gives its final approval, it should review the report thoroughly, even critically. Few things are of greater importance. Once officially adopted, the plan becomes the basis by which the organization's mission is accomplished.

Implementation Is Delegated

The planning group has completed its assignment. It should be thanked and dissolved. The board now delegates the approved plan to the administration for implementation. The board should incorporate several elements in the delegation process:

1. **Assure the administration of its confidence and support.** This is an opportunity to reinforce the partnership relationship which needs to exist between the board and the administration.

2. **Insure that the resources are available for plan implementation.** Few things are so demoralizing and counterproductive as to draw up ambitious plans and not be able to put them into action.

3. **Clarify the policies (and limitations) which are expected to guide program implementation.** Do they give the administration the guidance they need to meet board expectations?

4. **Provide for monitoring and evaluation.** Effective delegation involves both letting go and keeping in touch. Boards who do not let go of administrative detail demoralize staff and overburden themselves, often to the neglect of their governance function.

Boards who do not stay in touch are irrelevant to what is or is not happening and abdicate their responsibility. An appropriate middle position must be found.

The board is responsible to establish key performance indicators for major areas of activity. For example, in an effort to be an effective employer who seeks to foster personal growth, the board may adopt an objective that staff turnover should not exceed 10 percent per annum. Such a specific guideline helps the staff to know what is expected and by what standards its performance will be evaluated. It gives the board the confidence that it is doing its job.

An organization that is willing to learn puts considerable emphasis on evaluation. It strives continually to learn from its negative and positive experiences. The results of this ongoing evaluation are continually channeled back into and influence the administration and the planning process.

The board is able to evaluate an organization's workings in distinctly different ways than the administration can. Distance is often seen as a disadvantage, but it can also be an advantage in that it increases perspective. Being removed can increase objectivity. It can improve overall comprehension.

The purpose of evaluation, it should be recognized, is not to expose deficiencies. Instead, it is to determine that the mission and goals of the organization are being achieved in the most efficient and effective way possible.

"Plan to Plan II"

As the year comes to a close, the planning process comes full circle. A new effort begins to once again review the five-year plan, adding the new year and dropping the previous fifth year. The process begins with the board evaluating the year's performance against the plan which had been approved the previous year. It reviews its three-point Planning Foundations. It looks at its long-range goals and annual goals and makes a new projection. It makes a plan for its own board governance work and evaluates the procedures and policies by which the program implementation is delegated to the administration. An effective board always looks both back and ahead, deciding what it wants to do and how to go about doing it.

The tendency is for things which are done repeatedly to erode into meaningless routine. One antidote for this deadly temptation is to mandate a zero-based planning process every fifth year. Whereas routine planning proceeds from the base line, zero-based planning, as the term implies, is a new beginning.

Effective directors are always looking for ways to improve the performance of the organization which they have been elected to lead. To actively involve the directors in the ongoing planning process is one of the best ways to fulfill this responsibility.

Planning is a vital part of managing. Planning has been viewed as a systematic approach to steering an enterprise through the uncertain waters of a rapidly changing environment to accomplish mission. Why then does Tom Peters, the modern day management guru say, "The odds of success increase to the extent to which we let go of our master plan"?

He is not saying, do not plan. He is also not advocating taking the plan lightly. What he is saying is do not elevate your plan to holy writ. Do not hold it too rigidly. Do not freeze things in place at the very time that change is accelerating all around you. Do not assume that the plan will replace on-the-spot decision-making. To paraphrase an old proverb, plan your work, work your plan—and be prepared to amend your plan to take new needs and opportunities into consideration.

13.

CONFLICT:
Inevitable, and not necessarily bad

> *"Conflict is necessary and indispensable. There is no conflict only when no new decisions are made or no implementation of new decisions is necessary, which means death . . . Conflict is either destructive or constructive. It is never benign. It is constructive when it is functional; it is destructive when it is not channeled . . . What turns conflict into a destructive force is the lack of respect."*
> —Ichak Adizes in *Corporate Life Cycles*

CONFLICT IS the inevitable result of human interaction. Wherever two or three are gathered, there will be differences which may lead to conflict.

Some useful parallels can be drawn between conflict and fire. Fire is one of life's essentials. We need it to cook, to keep warm, to cleanse, and to smelt. But when fire rages out of control it becomes unfriendly and even deadly.

Conflict can, in the same way, serve a useful purpose. It is evidence of life, that people care, that they are sufficiently committed to something to be in conflict over it. Conflict is evidence that there is more than one way of doing something.

But like fire, conflict can become destructive. It can distract or even destroy an organization. In the heat of the United States' biggest civil conflict Abe Lincoln said, "A house divided against itself cannot stand." The challenge facing leaders everywhere is to respond to conflict in such a way as to produce a positive outcome.

It is useful to understand the conflict behavioral styles which play themselves out in boardrooms.

Conflict Behavioral Styles

1. **Competing:** Directors who are competitive are intent upon winning. They set things up so that they win or get their way, and anyone who opposes them loses. They ignore, conceal, or diminish information which does not support their predetermined conclusion. They are individualistic and decisive and thrive especially in crisis situations. Their style requires others to submit rather than to think creatively and independently.

2. **Accommodating:** Directors who are accommodating are quick to support what appears to be the prevailing point of view. They hesitate to oppose or seek other solutions. They dislike conflict intensely and are eager to arrive at a consensus. They want to be well liked by everyone.

3. **Avoiding:** Directors who are avoiding are clearly uncomfortable with any differing point of view. Because their first concern is to stay out of the crossfire of any dispute, they contribute little to finding the best solution. When the discussion heats up, they shut down.

4. **Compromising:** Directors who are compromising find consensus by combining those parts of a discussion on which there is agreement, in ways which are acceptable to the disputing parties. The art of compromise is part of the democratic process, and it has its place. Its limitation is that instead of working toward the best solution, it pulls the discussion toward the lowest common denominator. A compromised solution is often shallow and temporary.

5. **Collaborating:** Directors who are collaborating are first interested in identifying a variety of promising approaches to the

subject at hand. They invite debate and welcome all alternatives which strengthen the consensus which is emerging. Their interest is not so much in who wins and who loses, but in arriving at the best solution. The collaborative process takes longer, but the results are usually better and more enduring.

The first four behaviors are driven by self-interest. How can I win? How can I be liked? How can I avoid being embarrassed? Maybe I can be the hero by brokering a compromise. By way of contrast, collaborating directors are less self-interested and are first concerned with arriving at a conclusion which will best serve the cause.

The challenge of a board, and particularly its chair, is to create a trusting atmosphere where members feel sufficiently secure to express a differing or untested, but potentially promising, point of view. The focus should be on the issues, keeping turf and ego considerations out of it as much as is humanly possible. Some directors find this easier than others, but it is the goal towards which effective directors aspire.

Destructive Conflict Threatens Nevertheless

What should board members do when differences have gone beyond the bounds of constructive dialogue, and they are faced with the foreboding prospect of destructive conflict, including the threat of disintegration? There are many different kinds of conflict, and conflicts go through different stages, but some general principles may be useful:

Don't overreact. Some organizations are so idealistic that they view the mere threat of trouble as the sky falling in on them. Nonprofit organizations are especially prone to overreact when there is the threat of adverse publicity which may interfere with fund raising. Overreaction usually exacerbates the problem.

Organizations are remarkably tough. They can survive more adversity than is commonly recognized. Like ball players who are required to play through a slump, organizations need to keep functioning even when calamity threatens.

Own the problem–don't ignore it. This is your problem. It needs to be dealt with. Don't wish it away. Don't attempt to suppress it. However much you may regret it and however disruptive it may seem, view it as an opportunity to correct a weakness which has surfaced.

Fix it–yourself. Don't turn immediately to the outside. Remember that consultants don't make decisions for you–they help you to identify the options and their predicted consequences. Adversity is a time when leaders prove their mettle–and earn their nonprofit salary! More than ever, in a time of difficulty leaders must accept responsibility and exercise leadership. Failure to do so results in a vacuum which leads to rapid and unnecessary deterioration. Facts become confused with speculation and negative leadership may assert itself. In this situation leaders must do two things simultaneously.

First, they must have a thorough and accurate understanding of the situation. What is going on here? What is the problem? The real problem is often disguised by what turn out to be decoys. Leaders must maintain open minds and resolutely refuse to be pushed into action until they know the essential facts.

Second, while never attempting to suppress emotions, leaders manage the crisis in such a way that reason prevails over emotion. They do this best by demonstrating that leadership is functioning, by communicating openly, and by sharing the facts as they become available.

Once they know the facts, and before they make binding decisions, the board should consider its full range of options. It should not rush into a decision prematurely, but neither should it dally. It most assuredly should not procrastinate and shrink from a hard decision. It needs to shape a well developed proposal.

Seek outside help. Even as the doctor who treats himself has a fool for a patient, so there are situations where an organization must turn to the outside for help. Doing so may be a sign of strength. One such time may be when the leaders themselves are involved in the conflict, and they often are. Some may lament,

"Isn't this a sorry state of affairs we have fallen into?" Not necessarily. The sorry state may follow if help is not found.

Mediation is a form of conflict resolution being used increasingly in nonprofit and church settings. It is a process in which a trained and objective third party helps those in conflict find a mutually agreeable solution. The field of conflict resolution has grown to include mediation to resolve insurance claims, business disputes, and neighborhood conflicts. It also includes intra-group and organizational consulting in which a third party assists groups working through difficult situations. There are a wide variety of organizations and individuals who offer mediation and consulting services for individuals or groups in conflict. Many of these offer training in conflict resolution as well.

Our strong inclination is to avoid litigation, but not necessarily at all costs. It, too, is a form of conflict resolution, albeit a drastic and a costly one. For all its limitations, litigation is to be preferred over protracted conflict.

Grievance Procedure

Sometimes boards find themselves drawn into an administrative or personnel dispute. (Note the illustration on page 19 in Chapter 2 about a President who bypasses a Vice President to deal directly with a Department manager, and a Department manager who launches a complaint about the President to the board Chair.) Boards must not allow their energy and focus to be dissipated. A proactive board who works through policies will have a grievance procedure in place which insures evenhanded and fair treatment for everyone within the organization.

In the illustration sited above, the Chair (or another designated member of the board) should grant the requested interview only if the grievance procedure has not worked. (Even then she should be asking herself why it has not worked!) She should take a listening stance and refrain from coming to a quick conclusion. She must remind herself that this may not be a complete and objective account of what occurred and that there is surely more to the story.

Before the meeting is adjourned, the board member and staff person need to agree about how the information divulged in the meeting will be used. The board member should not speculate on the outcome of the situation; she can assure the staff person only that the allegations will be investigated appropriately.

The responsibility of the Chair now is to get the facts, to keep people appropriately informed, and to recommend appropriate action. Her first concern is justice; the second is damage control! If the order is reversed, neither is accomplished! Innocent parties can be severely and needlessly damaged by an inept handling of the situation, even if all involved have the best intentions.

The tendency for boards is to avoid conflict at all costs, and the cost of avoidance can be very high. The role of a board is not ceremonial; it is to solve problems that impede the organization's mission, and to recognize and seize opportunities that will enhance that mission. Even the most upstanding nonprofits frequently pass through times of conflict and misunderstanding. Only those boards that deal with it constructively experience the health that can follow.

We conclude by recalling a board meeting in a church setting where sharp differences had been expressed. Two men who were each deeply committed to the cause and independent in their thinking held on to what appeared to be irreconcilable differences. The time for adjournment came before agreement had been reached. One of the disputants was asked to offer a closing prayer. After a brief pause, he rose to the occasion with a beautiful, conciliatory prayer. I don't remember the full text of it, but it included the line, "Thank you for those who differ with us. They help us in ways that those who always agree with us never do."

14.

RENEWAL:
Preventing a premature death

> *"In an ever-renewing society, what matures is a system or a framework within which continuous innovation, renewal, and rebirth can occur."*
>
> –John W. Gardner

LIKE HUMANS, organizations have a limited life span. It is startling to realize that many organizations do not survive their founder by more than 10 years. Organizations, to draw on the biblical metaphor, spring up, they flourish for a time, then they linger and die. If organizations were given a formal burial like people, the graveyard would be enormous. The message of this chapter is that organizations can be renewed. Their useful life can be extended.

Remarkable recuperative powers are part of creation. My wife and I (Edgar) were living in Europe when CIBA-GEIGY accidentally spilled large quantities of poisonous chemicals into the Rhine River. Once the extent of the damage had been assessed, many believed that the Rhine was destined to be a dead body, good only for navigational purposes. Anyone who has lived on the banks of this beautiful, historic river knows how depressing that thought was. Newspapers daily traced the movement of the spill as it wove its way from Switzerland, through Germany and Holland, and finally out to the North Sea. On a visit four years later, we were pleased to learn that aquatic life was returning much sooner than had been thought possible. Renewal is an integral part of creation.

What is true of the physical world applies also to the world of sociology. Organizations wind down, and, if their mission is lost, they disappear. The United States of America, for all its problems, serves as a good illustration of a renewable system. Established more than 200 years ago, it has been racked by scandals of every kind. It seems always to be in the shadow of a looming crisis. But it has survived because its founders, in all their wisdom and after years of vigorous debate, put in place a system which is capable of self-correction. Contrast it, for example, with the Soviet Union which very quickly reached an extreme state of rigidity and which, after a mere 70 years, has disintegrated.

When asked, "What is the one most difficult thing that you personally need to work on?" Max DePree, chairman of the Herman Miller Company, said, "The interception of entropy." Unless deliberate care is given and action is taken, organizations run out of steam.

Many boards achieve spurts of genius, followed by embarrassing relapses. Some boards do not make the transition to the next stage as discussed in Chapter 1. Other boards get bogged down in mediocrity or conflict. Many get distracted, disenchanted, and bored. How can a board achieve sustained effectiveness?

The responsibility for board effectiveness is assigned to the chairperson. Many boards are not clear on this point. It is, we feel, improper to assign this function to the CEO or to permit him/her to act in this capacity. The board does not work for the CEO. The CEO works for the board and should not control it.

Practical Suggestions for Organizational Renewal

Review the organization's mission. Is it relevant? Is it focused? Is it bold? Most probing of all, do you believe in it?

The story is told of people living along a rocky coast in Nova Scotia where shipwrecks were a common occurrence. After a particularly sad tragedy, they mounted a campaign to build a lighthouse. The cause was urgent and people gave generously. Soon the lighthouse was in operation. Volunteers were recruited to staff it. When it became hard to recruit volunteers, staff was employed. Modern equipment was purchased. One year more money was collected than was needed for operations, so it was decided to equip the staff lounge so that off-duty workers could be more comfortable.

With the passage of time, coastal traffic decreased and ships were equipped with radar. The purpose for which the organization had been called into being had disappeared, but funds were available and old-timers had an emotional commitment to the cause. Leaders had failed to identify a new need, and thus the lighthouse effort continued for a time, even though no function was being served.

Organizations faced with low morale and disappointing fund drives should not be quick to conclude that the solution resides in a multicolor brochure or a more vigorous fund-drive chair. The deeper problem may be that the program has lost its relevance and urgency.

Review the people. "Organizations," observes John W. Gardner, "go to seed when the people in them go to seed. And they awaken when the people awaken. The renewal of organizations and societies begins with people." This may be either through enlisting new people or by the renewal of people already in the system. It must take place continuously at all levels of the organization, from entry level positions to career personnel to the board of directors.

For sustained effectiveness there needs to be some turnover in board membership. Deadwood should not be permitted. Board membership needs to change to reflect changing circumstances. Just as in plant life, where the bloom comes from the new growth, so new directors bring new life to an organization. They ask questions old directors are no longer asking. They attempt, and sometimes achieve, what old directors know is not possible.

Every board should, we believe, establish a maximum term of service that is between six and nine years. The problems that such a limitation brings are, in our experience, preferred to the problems and bad feelings which result when directors are allowed to assume election is for life. Term limits deliver the message that directors have limited time to make their contributions. The feelings of directors who have rendered many years of faithful service should not be disregarded, but neither should organizational effectiveness be sacrificed. (This subject is discussed in more detail in Chapter 15, "Leaving Right.")

New people bring new energy and new perspectives. They ask questions which persons who have been in the system no longer ask. A system is in trouble when it can no longer attract a stream of new talent.

Renewal happens when people have a future orientation, when they are driven by something they want to accomplish, when they care. Leaders can achieve renewal only if they believe in the possibility of it.

Review your plan. Does it commit you to specific goals? Are the identified goals challenging and are they achievable? Does your plan contain benchmarks against which to measure your progress or lack of it? Planning is one of the best ways a board has to exercise leadership and renewal.

Welcome change. "Bureaucracies," says Laurence Peter of Peter Principle fame, "defend the status quo long past the time when the quo has lost its status."

As organizations mature and achieve a measure of success, their tendency is to conserve, to live on the laurels of their past accomplishments. Like a basketball team with a history of success, organizations who are proud of their past may no longer dive for the loose ball. They hesitate to risk change. It is stated beautifully by Niccoló Machiavelli: "There is nothing more difficult to attempt, more perilous to conduct, or more uncertain in its success, than to take the lead in the introduction of a new order of things. Because the innovator has for enemies all those who have done well under the old conditions, and only lukewarm defenders in those who might do well under the new."

Learn from others. There is so much we can learn from others, and they are surprisingly willing to share it, if asked. Plan a retreat with a well chosen retreat person. Attend association meetings. Read relevant books and articles. Engage a consultant.

Evaluate your corporate culture. Does a positive spirit of teamwork prevail? Is there a commitment to excellence? Are relationships built on trust and mutual respect? Is it permissible to risk a new idea? Is the mission owned by all who are expected to contribute to it?

Organizations, like people, have their good times and their bad times. One experienced leader made the sage observation to his successor, "Things are usually not as good as they appear when they are up nor as bad as they appear when they are down."

When an organization is down, the temptation is to draw in, to retreat to a defensive position. Leaders, with the best of intentions, emphasize control and caution when vision and faith are most needed. The last act of an organization, it has been observed, is to enlarge the rule book. Its focus is on doing things right when it should be on doing the right things.

DePree reminds us that, "We cannot become what we need to be by remaining what we are." The renewing person, as well as the renewing organization, must be mature enough to be self-critical and admit, "We can do better." They must care enough to risk change.

15.

LEAVING RIGHT:
Signing off

> *"For everything there is a season—a time to engage and a time to disengage."*
>
> —A paraphrase from the
> Old Testament book of Ecclesiastes

LEAVING CAN BE a satisfying experience. A director has served well, and now the time has come to move on, making room for someone else to serve. It is a smooth and natural passage from something completed to something waiting. It is a time of reflection and thanksgiving. It is a cherished moment for both the retiring officeholder and those who remain to continue the work.

Leaving can also be a difficult time. Deep and meaningful relationships are not easily severed. Occasionally, persons leave boards feeling hurt and alienated from the very things they have worked so hard to build.

This should not be. This does not need to be. Organizations and their boards should give as much thought and planning to termination as they do to recruitment and orientation.

Expectations

In some organizations, a pattern exists whereby directors assume that unless they disgrace themselves, election is for as long as they want to serve. In an earlier generation those offices were sometimes conferred on directors' sons. It is not easy for a board to break this dynamic without hurting persons' feelings. Our advice to boards who find themselves in this situation is to be clear, be firm, be patient, and, above all, be loving. To paraphrase the Golden Rule, "Do unto retiring directors as you will want done unto you when the time comes." Leaving right involves as much thought and planning as installation. Organizations can act to make leaving easier and more positive.

1. Help directors to have realistic expectations, including the idea of a positive termination. Board service should be thought of as a task and privilege which rotates. The adoption of term and/or age limits guides directors as they subconsciously formulate their expectations. Mennonite Indemnity, a Mennonite church insurance service, has a covenant of board service in which directors pledge that when the time comes they intend to "step aside graciously and with goodwill to their successors and the cause."

2. Directors (and employees) should get frequent recognition for their contributions; such affirmation should not all be saved for retirement parties. The process of renomination to another term should be used as an opportunity to recognize what has been accomplished and to call for a new commitment. These moments can be handled in ways which reinforce the in (make your contribution)-and-out rhythm of board service.

3. There are special situations which call for flexibility. Even as directors are called upon to adjust their expectations when a new policy on board tenure is adopted, so boards must be flexible in how their ground rules are applied. When a board, for example, adopts a service maximum, directors affected by this change deserve some special consideration. Some boards in this situation

elect a director to a shorter term. Sometimes an extra year or two can be the difference between hurt or good feelings.

4. Ease the transition by providing for continued participation. A founding director, or someone who has served with distinction, may be given emeritus status. Someone with a unique gift or experience may be retained for a time as a consultant. Habitat for Humanity has a practice of electing former directors to the Board of Advisors and providing them with board meeting minutes for one year after their retirement. Many boards have a provision which permits directors to be brought back on the board after a year of leave.

Timing

Leaving right has a lot to do with timing. A director has found board service to be deeply satisfying and feels that she or he still has something unique to contribute. While many directors recall how some of their predecessors overstayed and vow not to do the same, privately they may entertain thoughts of indispensability. At least they may have grave doubts about the ability of young directors to uphold the proud tradition they have established and maintained. They see themselves now in that stage of life when they have more time for this type of service.

It is at such a moment that some directors get locked into a "one more term" syndrome. They may reluctantly hint at retirement, only to be greeted by a polite, "Oh, Jake, what would we do without you?" Jake makes a few disclaimers and after a brief pause says, "Okay, one more term." Later as the younger directors discuss it among themselves, one recalls that this was a repeat of what was said when Jake was up for reelection last time.

Directors who stay one term too long no longer enjoy the respect of their fellow directors. Although everyone is polite, they begin to hear the message—it's time to move on. Jake must admit to himself that there are more things that he doesn't understand and feel a part of. Once the dynamic has reached this stage, it is hard for a director to leave right.

To leave right, a director must leave at the right time. Sometimes this is not possible, but this should be the goal for both the director and the organization. But be forewarned—leaving right, even though it may be properly handled, is still not necessarily easy. We are reminded of a church leader who, upon losing a close election, said that turning the work over to his successor was more difficult than to have done it for 17 years.

Though this book is addressed specifically to directors, the concern for a positive termination applies equally to employees. They, no less than directors, have invested themselves in the cause and deserve appropriate recognition.

The importance of leaving right was brought home to me (Edgar) when a Mennonite Central Committee (MCC) overseas relief worker had an emotional breakdown which required her to return home for treatment. She responded well, but we were taken aback when the doctor advised that she be permitted to return to her former place of assignment so that she could "leave right." Didn't the doctor know or care that this meant expensive travel to a distant country? We allowed ourselves to be convinced, however, and in retrospect I feel MCC did what was owed this young church worker.

There are some things an organization can and should do to ease the adjustment of a retiring director, although some responsibility also resides with the director.

Leaving is inevitable. Leaving right is the last thing we should want after having contributed ourselves to a cause.

EXHIBIT 1

A More Excellent Way

We may speak the language of organizational structure and mission, but if we do not have love in our hearts for those who are intended to benefit from our efforts, they will have no more effect than a noisy gong or a clanging cymbal whose influence fades away with its clamor.

We may speak about Servant Leadership and clear lines of authority, we may have compelling strategies for organizational effectiveness and renewal, but if we have not love for people, it is all in vain. We may distribute our resources with the utmost efficiency and give our lives to save the world, but if love is not our motive, the world will be none the better for our effort.

With love we will be very patient and understanding as we interact with other cultures.

With love we will not feel boastfully righteous as though we have all the solutions to the world's needs.

With love we will never assert our superiority, never selfishly seek praise for sharing with others that with which we have been so abundantly blessed.

With love we will never inflate our ego at the expense of those we have come to serve.

With love we will always be slow to expose the failures and shortcomings of others.

With love we will not be resentful when our service is taken for granted.

Love never gives up. As for theories and strategies, they will be superseded; as for organizations, they will cease. For our planning and our institutions are incomplete, but when our actions are guided by love and justice, they will hit the mark.

We are limited in our understanding; we see in a mirror dimly. We are baffled by problems, and lasting solutions elude us. But we are learning bit by bit and we long for the day when love will rule the world.

Thus, faith that God has a plan for the world, hope that all can realize their human potential, and love that knows no boundaries–these three endure–but the greatest is love. Make love your goal.

–Edgar Stoesz, with gratitude to St. Paul (1 Corinthians 13).
Adapted from *Beyond Good Intentions* by Edgar Stoesz.

EXHIBIT 2

Duties of the Board of Directors
(A Job Description)

1. To identify the purpose for which the organization exists. What is its Mission? What does it commit itself to be and do?

2. To provide a plan by which the stated mission becomes operational:
   - long-range plan (3 to 5 years, reviewed and adjusted annually).
   - annual work plan, including measurable goals and budget.

3. To delegate implementation of the approved plans:
   - to either a committee or an administrative officer,
   - with applicable policies (instructions).

4. To safeguard the assets and future viability of the organization and to ensure the availability of resources needed to implement the approved plan.
   - **Personnel:** approve an organizational chart which clarifies reporting and authority relationships; salary and benefits scale; qualifications; provision for recruitment; provision for leadership succession.
   - **Finances:** institute accounting and fiscal procedures which comply with applicable laws and standard nonprofit accounting practices; provide for and review an independent audit; establish responsibility and plans for fund raising.

5. To monitor and evaluate:
   - its own board performance, and provide for continuity.
   - the performance of the Chief Executive Officer.
   - the program, with the CEO, to determine if the mission is being furthered as intended.

6. To provide accountability (reporting) to the membership.

EXHIBIT 2

Other documents which a board uses to do its work:
    the legal charter/articles of incorporation,
    the bylaws,
    the minute book,
    the compilation of board approved policies,
    the organizational chart,
    the long-range plan,
    the annual plan and budget.

EXHIBIT 3

Orientation of Board Members
A Checklist

Date of Orientation	Topic	Accountable Person
	1. Overview	**Board Chairperson**
_____	History, mission, values, goals of organization	
	2. Board Organization and Expectations of Board Members	**Board Chairperson**
_____	Job description for board members	
_____	Board meetings: time, place	
_____	Preparation: agenda, minutes	
_____	Committees: assignment	
_____	Annual board cycle: annual meeting, future plans	
_____	Planning cycle: policies, practices	
_____	Relation of board members and staff	
_____	Time expectations: meetings	
_____	Introduction to all other board members and their roles	
_____	Retreats	
_____	Recent annual evaluations of CEO	
_____	Financial commitments and reimbursements: meals, liability	
_____	Contributions, travel	
_____	Description of board responsibilities (read and understood)	
_____	Bylaws (read and understood)	
	3. Organization's Place in the Community	**Vice Chairperson**
_____	Industry, market	
_____	Competitors, collaborators	
_____	Reputation	

EXHIBIT 3

Date of Orientation	Topic	Accountable Person
	4. Financial Review	**Treasurer**
_____	Long-range financial plan	
_____	Fund raising	
_____	Balance sheet	
_____	Profit and loss: operations sheets	
_____	Budget procedures and current budget	
_____	Funding sources: problems, auditors	
	5. Description and Tour of Operations, Facilities	**CEO**
_____	Products, services	
_____	Clients	
_____	Methods of service distribution	
_____	Tour of facilities	
_____	Introduction to key or all staff	
_____	Organizational chart	
	6. Committee Assignment	**Committee Chairperson**
_____	Purpose of committee	
_____	Task of members	
_____	Arrangements/Meetings: time, place	
_____	Preparation of agenda, minutes	
_____	Individual assignment	
	7. Other	

I have completed this orientation and am sufficiently familiar with this organization to begin functioning as a board member with my assigned roles and tasks.

Signed_____ Date_____

EXHIBIT 4

Job Description for Board Chairperson

I. PRIMARY FUNCTION

The principal functions of the board chairperson are to lead and to facilitate the work of the board of directors and its relationship to the CEO.

II. RELATIONSHIPS AND PRACTICAL FUNCTIONS

A. To the board

1. Responsible to board. The chair is usually elected by the board and responsible to it for his/her work.
2. Leads board to develop long-term and annual goals and to achieve goals.
3. Convenes and presides at board meetings.
   a. Responsible to see that annual tasks are accomplished.
   b. Develops agenda and relevant materials to be circulated prior to meetings.
   c. Manages agenda and time in order to fulfill tasks in an efficient way.
   d. Assures that minutes are completed and sent immediately after all meetings.
   e. Seeks full participation of all members.
   f. Leads board in making sound decisions in order to fulfill the mission and goals of organization.
4. Communicates actions of board as necessary to assure implementation.

B. To the vice chairperson

1. In his/her absence, the chair will delegate powers and tasks to the vice chair.
2. The vice chair should be informed frequently of the chair's work and concerns so that the vice chair can substitute for the chair with minimal loss and stress.
3. May assign key tasks to the vice chair, such as designating committee chairs.

EXHIBIT 4

C. To the Chief Executive Officer

1. The chair works closely with the CEO to define the CEO's responsibilities, goals, and extent of his/her authority in a written job description. The CEO is accountable for all his/her work to the board, communicated through the board chair. (This is apart from the staff report which the CEO makes to the whole board.)
2. The chair conveys and interprets the values, goals, plans, concerns, and actions of the board to the CEO whenever such clarification is needed.
3. The chair conducts regular meetings with the CEO to keep abreast of important organizational issues (personnel, financial condition, progress on goals) and the personal needs of the executive (vacations, professional development, staff relationships, job satisfaction, intentions about continuing in the position).
4. The chair and CEO meet following the CEO's annual report to evaluate the CEO's work during the preceding year and to assist the CEO in the setting of personal, professional, and organizational goals for the next year.
5. The chair communicates annually with the board, and then the CEO about the CEO's compensation.
6. The chair maintains a close relationship with the CEO, so that the board is assured that the CEO is fulfilling their expectations and so that the CEO has someone with whom he/she can discuss the working situation.

D. To the public(s)

1. The chair is the board's spokesperson to its various publics, the press, and other media if board expression is advisable. Board members should not speak individually on behalf of the board unless assigned to do so by the chair.
2. The chair and CEO should confer before meeting the publics and support each other in that process.
3. The chair may represent the organization at various functions in coordination with the CEO.
4. The chair in his/her daily activities endeavors to listen carefully to public opinion about the organization and seeks the goodwill of others toward the organization.
5. In general, the chair is to watch over the total life and development of the organization, so that it is meeting genuine human needs and fulfilling its mission.

EXHIBIT 5

Annual Calendar of Board Tasks

This is a suggested calendar of board tasks. A board may identify different tasks but should coordinate them with its own meeting schedule.

1. Review the mission, values, and philosophy of management of the organization.

   —Mid-year

2. Set goals for the organization, both annual and long-term.

   —2-6 months prior to beginning of Fiscal Year (FY)

3. Approve plans of action proposed by the CEO by which the organization will achieve the goals set by the board.

   —1-3 months prior to beginning of FY

4. Financial: approve budget(s)—capital and operating—contributions, etc. Review investments, policies, procedures, results, changes, and borrowings.

   —1-3 months prior to beginning of FY

5. Establish regular meeting procedure and schedule for board and committees to accomplish goals.

   —Mid-year

6. Organize the board in order to achieve the goals of the board:
   A. Committees
   B. Task Forces
   C. Consultants
   D. New members

   —According to the schedule outlined by the board

7. Monitor the progress of the management and company toward its goals through reports from the CEO, board committees, financial reports, and key staff.

   —At each board meeting

EXHIBIT 5

8. Orientation for new board members:
   A.   to each other,
   B.   to the task of being a board member,
   C.   to the organization,
   D.   to the key staff,
   E.   to the organization's goals, values, needs, problems, etc.
            –Immediately after new members are appointed

 9. Identify the most urgent issues calling for board attention and make a
    plan for how they will be addressed.
            –1-3 months prior to beginning of FY

10. Plan and conduct continuing education of board.
            –Early in the new year

11. Identify and make provision to supply information useful to the related
    publics (stakeholders) and provide for appropriate interaction,
    including annual reports, new program materials, announcements, etc.
            –Throughout the year

12. Review and evaluate annual report of the CEO. (This report should
    include financial, operations, and personnel reports.)
      –2-3 months after close of FY, when annual report is complete

13. Self-evaluation of board performance.
            –2-3 months after close of FY

EXHIBIT 6

General Outline for Board Committee Accountability

A board may appoint whatever committees it chooses, subject to its own bylaws. Each committee should be given a written assignment, following or adapted from this general outline:

1. Name of committee
2. Committee membership
3. Staff liaison
4. Purpose
5. Duties and responsibilities
6. Reporting procedures/schedule
7. Committee budget
8. Projected schedule of meetings

Additional considerations:

1. The purpose (#4) of the board committee is to help the board (not the administrator) do its work. Board committees study specific issues as assigned to them by the board (not the CEO), identify options, and draw up recommendations for board action. They do pre-board–not sub-board–work. It is important to recognize that the only authority a committee has is that which is assigned to it by the board.

2. The duties and responsibilities (#5) of board committees are assigned by the board annually in a manner so that the whole board and senior staff know what issues are being addressed. Individual committees should identify the specific issues they plan to address, but those suggestions are subject to board approval and should likewise be shared with the entire board and senior staff.

EXHIBIT 6

3. Reporting (#6). Items that a committee brings that require action should be presented in written form. This is sometimes difficult because committees often meet immediately prior to a board meeting.

A recommendation which has implications for departments which did not participate in its formation should be available for discussion before the recommendation is presented to the board for action. This may mean that the recommendation is given a first reading at the next meeting. This slows down the decision-making process, but when these steps are not taken, it is frequently necessary for a board to reconsider an action. This pacing is less objectionable when we recognize that we are dealing here with Ends issues and not administrative detail which needs immediate action.

The reporting should include a summary of the factors which led to the conclusion. When this is not done, boards often feel the need to redo the work of the committee.

EXHIBIT 7

A Performance Appraisal of the Chief Executive Officer

The purpose of this appraisal is to give support to the CEO, to clarify mutual expectations, to assess progress on agreed upon plans, and to identify areas for improvement, together with a plan to resolve them.

Who conducts the appraisal? The chair, sometimes with another board member present, or a committee of the board, who report to the board. A consultant may be engaged to help a board introduce this procedure or conduct it if there are special circumstances, but this should not be necessary routinely.

When? As mutually agreed, preferably early in the year, but annually.

Where? As agreed, but in a private office, not a public restaurant, and free of interruptions.

Preparation? The date and procedure should be agreed upon well in advance.

Procedure? The board chair or the committee chair is in charge, although the process should be interactive. All parties should be asked to reserve two hours for the interview. The CEO's job description and the summary of previous reviews form the beginning point. The review should be positive, while also being honest and realistic. Sensitive points should not be avoided. If there are specific grievances or points of dissatisfaction by either party, they should be discussed in detail, seeking also for resolution. the conclusions should be summarized in writing and form the basis for the next evaluation.

EXHIBIT 7

The Board Chair, or the chair of a special board committee in consultation with the Board Chair, should check her/his appraisal of the CEO's work over the past fiscal year, using the following descriptions:

A = Outstanding
B = Expected
C = Below Expectation
D = Unacceptable

1. PLANNING

A B C D

__ __ __ __ A. The CEO works with the board to develop and implement a planning process that guides the organization into long-term and continued growth and that guides it toward achieving the larger mission of the organization.

__ __ __ __ B. The CEO uses a long-range and annual planning process that involves the managers and supervisors in the organization. (This is directly aimed at accomplishing the goals established by the board of directors.)

__ __ __ __ C. The CEO uses a budgeting process (with department participation) that involves annual and monthly targets for capital, income, and expense items.

__ __ __ __ D. The CEO brings annual plans and budgets for accomplishing the goals of the organization to the board for approval on the agreed upon schedule.

__ __ __ __ E. The CEO develops (so that the board can approve) policies and procedures that effectively help guide and designate actions of the staff toward the goals.

II. ORGANIZING

A B C D

__ __ __ __ A. The CEO has developed and leads an organizational structure that is consistent with the organization's management philosophy and is effective in accomplishing its goals.

__ __ __ __ B. The CEO has developed and supports a development program for all employees that is preparing the organization for the future.

__ __ __ __ C. The organization has the most highly qualified, trained, and productive staff possible with a satisfactory turnover ratio.

III. LEADING

A B C D

__ __ __ __ A. The CEO has an excellent communication system established in all areas of the organization, assuring adequate communication from anyone to anyone.

__ __ __ __ B. The CEO has a well developed performance appraisal system working in the organization which begins with an annual performance plan for each person.

__ __ __ __ C. The CEO understands how people are motivated toward work and is an effective leader in helping them to contribute their best to accomplishing the work of the organization. (This builds morale.)

EXHIBIT 7

IV. CONTROLLING

A B C D

___ ___ ___ ___ A. At the end of the year, income and expense budgets are within guidelines established at the beginning of the year.

___ ___ ___ ___ B. Effective supervisory processes are at work within the organization, resulting in:
1. accomplishing goals;
2. employees learning and growing;
3. annual or more frequent performance appraisals;
4. monthly or more frequent private communication with each employee by supervisor;
5. strong teamwork.

V. RELATIONSHIPS

A B C D

___ ___ ___ ___ A. The CEO has an effective relationship with community people, which assists the organization in accomplishing its goals.

___ ___ ___ ___ B. The CEO has an effective relationship with the board of directors, which assists the organization in accomplishing its goals.

___ ___ ___ ___ C. The CEO has an effective relationship with his/her immediate staff and all employees, which assists the organization in accomplishing its goals.

___ ___ ___ ___ D. The CEO has an effective relationship with customers and clients, which assists the organization in accomplishing its goals.

VI. OVERALL

A B C D

___ ___ ___ ___ A. The CEO provides leadership for the organization's total activities that succeed in accomplishing the goals as established by the board of directors.

EXHIBIT 8

Annual Board Self-Assessment

INTRODUCTION

This procedure is intended first to help board members to be aware of their total task and, secondly, to insure that they are accomplishing that task. This approach may be altered to suit the circumstances of an individual organization, but some type of systematic evaluation procedure can help increase a board's effectiveness.

SUGGESTED PROCEDURE

1. The Board Self-Assessment is placed on the agenda of a future board meeting, and time is reserved accordingly. (This process does not need to be annual, but should be done every several years.)

2. The subject is introduced by the chair, who emphasizes its importance and explains what should be done with the evaluation form. Provision should be made for absent directors to participate.

3. Board members may complete the form while the meeting is in session and return them to the designated person—the chair, secretary, or chair of Board Services Committee—or take them home and return them in a few days.

4. The results are tabulated, summarized, reproduced, and distributed to the members.

5. Time is reserved at the next board meeting to discuss the issues that emerged from these assessments, placing them in order of priority and assigning them for appropriate follow-up.

EXHIBIT 8

Annual Board Self-Assessment

Instructions: Check "Yes," "No," or "Unc." (uncertain). Add ideas, questions, actions needed under "Notes."

	YES	NO	UNC.	NOTES
ACTIVITIES				
1. The board understands that its accountability includes financial responsibility, accounting and control, and social/ethical decisions.				
2. Good printed materials about the organization are available in an attractive and up-to-date format, and publicity appears in appropriate media in sufficient frequency and quality.				
3. The board represents the organization to the public, giving reports and listening to public needs and concerns.				
4. The board approves selection of outside counsel (attorney).				
RELATION TO CHIEF EXECUTIVE OFFICER				
5. The board selects a Chief Executive Officer and delegates to him/her full responsibility for all duties, except those reserved for the board.				
6. The board establishes an annual performance plan for the Chief Executive Officer and monitors and evaluates annually.				

	YES	NO	UNC.	NOTES
7. The board has a succession plan for the Chief Executive Officer and other designated key officers.				
8. The board recognizes the importance of the Chief Executive Officer's physical, mental, spiritual, and social health, and commissions the board chairperson to address these matters specifically and sensitively with the CEO.				
APPROVES MISSION, POLICIES, GOALS, AND PLANS				
9. The mission, purpose, and values of the organization are clearly defined and approved by the board.				
10. The board consistently focuses its attention and time on "Ends" matters–mission fulfillment, goal achievement, and values–rather than on operations and procedures.				
11. The board holds itself responsible for the strategic and long-term plans for the organization and gives time each year to address, update, and monitor those plans.				
12. The board approves an annual operations plan each year.				
13. General operating policies, personnel policies, and job descriptions are in writing, are easily accessible (in binder format), and are regularly updated.				

EXHIBIT 8

	YES	NO	UNC.	NOTES
14. The organization meets all laws, regulations (local, state, national, international), and licensing or accreditation standards above and beyond the bare minimum required, including quality and safety.				
MONITORS FINANCIAL STRUCTURE AND ACTIVITY				
15. The board approves all changes in capital structure.				
16. The board approves an income and expense budget in line with policy.				
17. The board approves and monitors all long- and short-term borrowing.				
18. Insurance coverage for board, staff, facilities, programs, etc. is monitored regularly.				
19. The board authorizes an annual independent financial audit and reviews the report with the auditor.				
20. The board authorizes all bank signatures.				
21. The board oversees all fund-raising activities.				
22. The board establishes financial procedures which are completely and accurately followed, including billing, accounts management, accounting, taxes, etc.				

	YES	NO	UNC.	NOTES
MONITORS, REVIEWS, AND APPRAISES MANAGEMENT				
23. The board approves the operational/organizational relationships, or changes departments, divisions, and lines of accountability as needed.				
24. The board reviews and approves compensation for key staff and a compensation plan for the total organization.				
25. The board approves company benefit plans, pensions, profit sharing, stock plans, etc., or exceptions to plans as applicable.				
MONITORS PERFORMANCE OF MANAGEMENT				
26. The board receives and monitors–at least quarterly–financial, statistical, and operations reports.				
27. The board reviews and critiques staffs' deficiencies in performances and assists in remedies.				
RESPONSIBLE FOR MANAGEMENT OF THE BOARD				
28. The board operates with a clear and current set of bylaws with which all board members are familiar.				
29. Roles and responsibilities of board and committees are well defined and understood, with descriptions for each.				

EXHIBIT 8

	YES	NO	UNC.	NOTES
30. The board provides for removal of board members for just cause; e.g., missing more than 20% of board meetings without excuse.				
31. New board members receive orientation in all aspects of the board's work.				
32. The board creates committees of the board, defines their functions, and dissolves them as appropriate.				
33. The board has an executive committee to handle matters which may come up between meetings. Its authority is specified in the bylaws.				
34. Training for board work is a regular part of its annual plan.				
35. A procedure for appraisal of the board and individual member's performance is done regularly.				
BOARD MEETINGS				
36. All members actively participate in each meeting of the board and committees to which they are assigned.				
37. The board has an effective procedure for decision-making which it follows; all appropriate persons are involved in the process. Board meetings are effective.				
38. The board has executive sessions (without staff) regularly.				

	YES	NO	UNC.	NOTES
39. The board has a regular report from the chair, as well as a report from the CEO.				
40. Agenda and other board materials, including study documents, are mailed to members in sufficient time for review in advance of board meetings.				
41. Board and committee minutes are circulated to members soon after each meeting.				
42. There is a clear separation of board functions and responsibilities from management functions and responsibilities.				
43. Major proposals are thoroughly processed before they are presented and are available in written form.				

EXHIBIT 9

Legal Dimensions:
The Risks Involved in Doing Good

> *"No obstacle [to volunteer service] is more chilling than the fear of personal liability and the high cost of insurance to protect against liability."*
>
> —George Bush

Board service has long been seen as a duty and an honor, and so it is. It is one way in which persons who have achieved a level of success are able to make their talents available to the wider community. The value of services given in this way is inestimable.

There has been, in recent years, an erosion of charitable immunity. Directors serve under the possibility of personal liability. As society has become more litigious, the exposure has extended from the for-profit to the nonprofit sector. Today, both are held to the same standard of conduct.

Each person is expected to be responsible and to act in a reasonable manner which does not harm others. When a person accepts service on a board, he or she assumes the responsibility for directing and managing the affairs of an organization and is expected to act in a certain way. Thus, each director and officer should prepare to assume some level of personal risk which unavoidably accompanies such service.

Directors and officers (D&O) should not be paranoid about this liability, but neither should they be naive about it. Directors obviously have self-interest in maintaining their personal assets. They are also responsible to direct as many organizational resources (financial, human, etc.) as possible toward accomplishing the mission and goals of the organization, rather than paying indemnity or excessive D&O insurance premiums. This is vital to good stewardship.

Wrongful Acts as Sources of Liability

Liability generally occurs when there is an injury or harm caused by a wrongful act. The party responsible for causing the injury is made to pay the costs.

D&O liability has to do with wrongful acts committed by directors and officers. The term "wrongful acts" is defined technically as "any negligent act, error, commission, breach of duty, misstatement, misleading statement, or other act done or willfully attempted by the directors or officers acting in their capacities as such." Thus, a director or officer must have acted or failed to act according to some standard of care which is expected of directors and officers.

Thus, wrongful acts need not be willful wrongdoing. They may, in fact, be ever so innocent or, at times, may even seem unavoidable. The following illustrations depict the types of circumstances which can confront nonprofit organizations:

Grievance: A board moves to terminate an employee for what appears to be "just cause." Later the fired employee contends that her civil rights were violated and her professional career damaged. Suit is brought and the board and organization are made to defend themselves.

Moral Impropriety: An employee is found to be engaging in sexual misconduct. A parent of one of the victims brings suit, contending that serious psychological damage has been done to his child. In the investigation, it is discovered that the charged employee has a record of similar offenses, but the pre-employment screening procedure had not been sufficiently thorough to discover it. The organization is made to defend itself against the charge of negligence.

Preventive Maintenance: A fire kills two elderly nursing home residents. In the investigation it is learned that a few months earlier a mechanical engineering firm evaluated the physical plant. The report which was submitted to the board warns that some equipment is unreliable and needs to be replaced. Carelessness is alleged.

These examples demonstrate that the board is responsible to monitor and manage the risks to which the organization and each director or officer is subject. The board, each director, officers, and CEO, therefore, should periodically engage in a process of: (1) identifying and analyzing risks, (2) selecting and implementing risk prevention programs, and (3) allocating the costs in the event that there is a loss. This should be done with the help of an attorney who can explain what legal risks the directors and officers and the organization face. Also, an attorney can assist in developing and implementing a risk-prevention program for the directors and officers. After identifying and assessing the risks and the likelihood of a loss, it is important to determine how the responsible party will pay the loss if one should occur.

EXHIBIT 9

Risk Identification and the Standard of Care

When identifying risks, it is important to determine how D&O liability might be imposed and who the injured party might be. Generally, D&O liability can be imposed upon a director when there is an injury caused by: (1) the breach of some standard of care, (2) the violation of a statute, or (3) the application of strict liability. Having identified the cause of the injury, it is important to identify the injured party.

The Standards of Care, Loyalty, and Obedience

Traditionally, directors and officers have duties of care, loyalty, and obedience which are owed to the organization and each other. Although these specific duties may be expressed in different terms from state to state, directors and officers are expected to exercise their duties in good faith, in a manner which is reasonably believed to be in the best interests of the organization, and with the care exercised by an ordinarily prudent person.

The duty of care or diligence implies extending the care that a reasonably prudent person in a similar position would use under similar circumstances. Prior to making a business decision, directors or officers should inform themselves of all material information reasonably available to them. This can be demonstrated by taking the time necessary, on an ongoing basis, to understand the operations and finances of the organization.

The duty of loyalty is based upon acting in good faith and in the best interests of the organization. Thus, directors and officers are required to refrain from engaging in personal activities which may injure or take advantage of the organization. They are prohibited from using their positions of trust and confidence to further their private interests. This duty requires an undivided and unselfish loyalty to the organization and demands that there be no conflict between one's duty to the organization and self-interest.

The duty of obedience requires directors and officers to perform their duties in accordance with applicable statutes and the terms of the organization's charter. Directors and officers may be liable if they authorize an act which is beyond the powers conferred upon a corporation by its charter or by applicable federal or state law. A breach of any of these duties will generally injure the organization or the fellow directors and officers. Thus, the organization and fellow directors and officers can bring suit against a director and officer.

Statutory or Strict Liability

Some statutes will hold a director liable for certain acts or omissions of the organization. Federal income tax law, the Employee Retirement Income

Security Act (ERISA), and environmental laws contain provisions which can hold a director liable in certain cases.

Third Party Liability

A director or officer may be named in a lawsuit by the mere fact that he or she is a director or officer. These lawsuits are generally known as third party suits and involve personal injury or damage to property. In these suits, a third party (i.e., not a director, officer, or member of the organization, nor the state attorney general) is injured by either the organization or by an agent acting within the scope of his or her duties. The third party can seek to recover damages from the organization and, in doing so, may even name the directors individually in the lawsuit.

Generally, the corporation, and not the directors and officers, will be liable for these injuries. The organization's general liability and property insurance policies should cover these costs.

To add clarity to this subject and restore some aspects of charitable immunity, some states have enacted laws which provide volunteer directors and officers and volunteer workers with immunity. This immunity, however, is provided to a director, officer, or volunteer for acts which are not intentional, wanton, or grossly negligent. Despite this statutory immunity, and regardless if the director, officer, or volunteer are ultimately liable, a person can still be named in a suit which requires defending oneself.

Risk Assessment

There are many techniques for assessing the risk associated with D&O liability. In determining which technique(s) to use, it is important to perform an assessment of the likelihood of a loss and the amount of the loss if it should occur (including the legal costs associated with a defense of a lawsuit).

1. **Avoidance.** Some risks of D&O liability can be eliminated entirely by not engaging in hazardous activity. A hospital board may refuse to authorize certain types of high risk treatment which avoids exposing the hospital and the board to the risk of liability. Liability, therefore, may be a factor in deciding if a new service should be initiated.

2. **Reduction.** The degree of risk can be materially reduced through loss control procedures. Some boards require each director and officer to identify on an annual basis significant and other interests which could pose conflicts of interest. The board would know ahead of time when there is a potential conflict of interest by one of its members.

Also, it is wise for a board to conduct an annual orientation for new and

EXHIBIT 9

existing board members so that they are thoroughly knowledgeable about the activities of the organization and the board's responsibilities. Most boards require that their organizations' financial and other pertinent information be submitted to them on a regular basis and prior to each board meeting so that each director and officer can be prepared to discuss the issues. Adequate minutes of meetings which document the discussions and activities can reduce exposure.

3. **Separation.** A multifaceted nonprofit organization may create a separate corporation for one of its more hazardous activities, and thus insulate the host organization and its directors and officers from liability. It does not reduce the potential liability of the board of the separate corporation. Each board should use similar risk management techniques.

4. **Retention.** An organization may choose to be self-insured on at least some of its risk through the election of a deductible and through the limits of the insurance. This may take the form of creating a self-insurance fund which, as it grows, makes possible an increased deductible and lower limits. Note should be taken of the fact that self-insurance is not synonymous with "going bare." To the extent the organization is unable to meet its obligations through insurance or its resources, each director and officer may face potential liability and may be retaining some risk.

5. **Transfer.** The costs can be transferred by a contract. This is usually done through the purchase of insurance, but it can also take the form of indemnification which can be provided by law or by contract.

Indemnification for Directors and Officers

Many states have adopted legislation which permits nonprofit organizations to indemnify or reimburse directors and officers for amounts they may be called upon to pay to satisfy a judgment brought against them in their capacities as directors or officers or money spent on their legal defenses. Some states have permissive indemnification, which means the organization has some discretion and must decide to provide the indemnification through a provision in the articles of incorporation, bylaws, or resolution, or through a separate agreement with each director or officer. Other states have mandatory indemnification which provides that a director is entitled by law to indemnification when certain statutory conditions have been met. Also, if state law permits it, organizations should consider advancing defense costs.

The indemnification provision is useful, but, in and of itself, it is not adequate protection for directors and officers. First, it is limited in its application. Indemnification is improper if the directors or officers breach their duties as stated in this chapter. Personal liability for fines or punitive damages may not be indemnified because of the public interest in holding individuals responsible when they willfully violate established rules. Finally, the indemnification provision is only as good as the resources an organization has to make good on its agreement to reimburse.

The organization, therefore, should consider obtaining a directors and officers liability insurance policy, because the policy covers the wrongful acts of the directors and officers and the indemnification which an organization may be required to pay. This policy strengthens the indemnification provision in that it expands the resources an organization has available to it.

What You Are Buying When You Buy D&O Insurance

In addition to indemnification, directors and officers can also transfer the costs of liability through the purchase of insurance. Insurance policies have deductibles, exclusions, and limits which means that the transfer is partial. If the policy limits are reached, then the directors and officers or the organization (if indemnification is in effect) must cover the loss.

A D&O insurance policy generally contains two parts to its coverage: (1) the policy covers errors and omissions of the directors and officers; and (2) the policy covers amounts the organization is obligated to pay directors and officers because of indemnification. D&O liability insurance does not cover liability for personal injuries or property damage which are generally third party actions and covered under a general liability policy.

The insuring agreement protects an organization with respect to its indemnification and the directors and officers with respect to "loss" arising from claims lodged against them by reason of a "wrongful act." "Loss" is generally defined as including costs, charges, and expenses incurred in the defense of actions, suits, or proceedings. The usual coverage is fairly broad, but there are a number of standard exclusions which normally include: (1) libel and slander; (2) benefits obtained through personal gain; (3) unlawful distributions; and (4) dishonesty. Bodily injury, property damage claims, pollution claims, and intra-board suits are also common exclusions. Some of these claims would be a part of the general liability or property insurance policies.

Careful attention should be given to whether the policy is written on an occurrence or a claims-made basis. With occurrence coverage, an incident is covered if it occurs within the policy period. Coverage under a claims-made policy depends on the claim being filed during the policy period. If a claim is not filed until a specified later date, the claim may not be honored.

It is important to establish that the policy being bought includes a provision for defense. First, defense is where the major expenses occur. A sur-

EXHIBIT 9

vey the Wyatt Company took in 1988 revealed that 60% of all claims were closed without payment to the claimant. The same study revealed that the average time lag from claim to disposition was 5.25 years. A defense, even against what may appear to be a frivolous charge, can be very expensive. Second, the value of insurance is not only in the ability to pay, but also in the experience and expertise an insurance company has to put together in a good defense. Some organizations feel that defense is one of the most important provisions within an insurance policy.

Prevention by the Organization

It is important to implement a risk prevention program in conjunction with the insurance purchased. This program demonstrates to donors and volunteers that an organization is concerned about good stewardship. In addition, the better the loss record (i.e., the fewer the losses), the less likely that insurance premiums will increase substantially.

The likelihood of wrongdoing by directors and officers can be reduced by the adoption of good board meeting procedures. Meetings should be held regularly and in a businesslike atmosphere. Ample time should be allowed to deal with complex issues. The agenda and background papers should be distributed well in advance of the meetings. Minutes should not only record actions, but they should also summarize the major considerations which went into decisions. The results of all votes taken should be recorded, along with the names of directors who voted against an action. In a particularly crucial situation, it may be in order to ask legal counsel to review the minutes before they are approved.

Written procedures and instructions on a variety of sensitive administrative subjects, i.e., grievance procedures, sexual misconduct, etc., can reduce wrongdoing and strengthen the defense if legal action is brought. The key to any risk prevention program is to follow through with the implementation of the policies and procedures which reduce the risk of liability. Additionally, it is vital to document continued adherence to the program in the minutes and corporate records.

Prevention by Individual Directors and Officers

There are things which individual directors and officers can do to enhance their performances and, at the same time, reduce the likelihood of wrongdoing:

1. Directors should attend all board and pertinent committee meetings.
2. Directors should demonstrate good faith; they must meet the prudency test.

3. Newly elected/appointed directors and officers should acquaint themselves with the bylaws, the mission statement, employment manuals, and written statements of policy and procedure. It is also wise for them to read the minutes of the board meetings held in the previous year or two.

4. Each director should identify conflicts of interest when such is known to exist and should decline to participate in a decision where conflict of interest can be alleged.

5. If the organization does not have directors' and officers' liability insurance, it may be possible for individual directors to have limited coverage endorsed onto their homeowners policies.

6. Any director casting a negative vote on a resolution which is adopted should be so recorded in the minutes.

7. Directors and officers who are not comfortable with procedures and actions should consider resigning if they are unable to gather adequate support for changes which they believe are necessary.

Conclusion

D&O insurance extends to the liability of the directors and officers in performance of their duties (of care, loyalty, and obedience). It also covers an organization for whatever it pays out pursuant to indemnification. The insurance does not otherwise cover an organization's liabilities which are subject to a commercial general liability policy. One of the benefits of D&O insurance is that legal defense costs are covered. Thus, if there is a possibility that a director or officer will be sued, D&O insurance helps to cover the legal costs and expenses incurred.

Each organization should be concerned with stewardship of resources. An organization should avoid subjecting any person to an unnecessary risk of loss. This can be done with a good risk prevention program and insurance, if appropriate.

Directors and officers should not be paranoid, but neither should they be naive. They should, if they believe in the cause they have been elected to represent, be prepared to assume some level of risk which unavoidably accompanies their service.

For the information contained in this chapter, we gratefully acknowledge the collaboration of Peter Beard who served as the corporate attorney for Habit for Humanity until 1993.

EXHIBIT 10

Organizational Proverbs

1. *I would hate to be an opportunity in the presence of some boards.*

2. *Majority rules, but is it wise?*
   The Bible pictures the majority as on the broad, well traveled road that leads to destruction. Robert Frost took the road less traveled–and it made all the difference.

3. *The only thing worse than majority rule is minority rule.*
   The sheep sleep while the wolves scheme.

4. *Just because decisions are arrived at democratically, doesn't mean they are wise.*
   Some of the worst decisions I participated in were unanimous. Richard Nixon won reelection by a landslide just months before he was driven from office in disgrace.

5. *Wisdom is not always on the side of caution.*
   In the biblical story of the talents, the loser was the one afraid to risk.

6. *According to your faith be it unto you.*
   If you believe that you can, and have a plan to achieve it, you can. If you don't believe that you can, you most assuredly can't. According to your faith be it unto you.

7. *According to your fund raising be it unto you.*
   Big league organizations are big league fund raisers; you have it only to the extent that you can raise it.

8. *The future belongs to those who plan for it.*
   Planning, be it formal or informal, be it long-ranged or short-ranged, is an act of faith.

9. *No raw meat.*

    Actions must be "pre-cooked." If an Executive or a committee brings an issue which has not been properly processed for action, send it back to the kitchen.

10. *Wine ages, bread rises, tea steeps, hams cure, but meeting planners are inclined toward the microwave approach—they zap and serve.*

11. *The new growth produces the bloom.*

    It is as true of boards as of plants. Freshmen add a valuable dimension. They ask questions seniors no longer ask, and aren't always satisfied with the answers given.

12. *Average boards orient themselves around the rearview mirror—precedent is the big thing. Good boards examine everything under the microscope— they want to avoid mistakes. Great boards look through a telescope to the planets beyond—at what could be.*

    –Edgar Stoesz

Recommended Readings

Adizes, Ichak.
1988 *Corporate Life Cycles.* Englewood NJ: Prentice Hall.
A detailed explanation of how organizations grow or do not grow, focusing on the needs of the organization itself.

Carver, John.
1990 *Boards That Make a Difference.* San Francisco: Jossey-Bass.
This is a sophisticated, doctrinaire book that is quite useful to mature boards or boards that want to lead their organization and themselves to maturity.

Carver, John and Miriam Mayhew Carver.
1996 *Basic Principles of Policy Governance.* San Francisco: Jossey-Bass Publishers.
A complete governance model complete with seven principles of governance and a nine-step plan for implementation.

DePree, Max.
1989 *The Art of Leadership.* New York: Dell Publishing.
An inspirational description of participative management in a very successful for-profit business that nonprofits should learn from.

Drucker, Peter F.
1990 *Nonprofit Management and Leadership, Vol. 1.* San Francisco: Jossey & Bass.

Eadie, Douglas C.
Beyond Strategic Planning. National Center for Nonprofit Boards, 2000 L Street NW, Suite 411, Washington DC, 20036.

Fisher, Roger and William Ury.
1981 *Getting to Yes.* Boston: Houghton-Mifflin Co.
Practical steps to negotiating everything from everyday family decisions to corporate strategies.

Greenleaf, Robert.
1977 *Servant Leadership.* New York: Paulist Press.
Practical implications and methods for "If any one among you would be chief, let him be the servant of all."

Hesselbein, Frances, Marshall Goldsmith, and Richard Beckhard, editors.
1996 *The Leader of the Future.* San Francisco: Jossey-Bass Publishers.
New visions, strategies, and practices for the next era.

Kotter, John P.
1990   *A Force for Change.* New York: The Free Press.
A useful description of the difference and need for leadership as compared to management.

Lai, Mary L.
Am I Covered? Consortium for Human Services, Box 1183, San Jose, CA, 95108.

Leas, Speed B.
Moving Your Church Through Conflict. Alban Institute, 4125 Nebraska NW, Washington DC, 20016.

Mueller, Robert K.
Smarter Board Meetings: For Effective Board Governance. National Center for Nonprofit Boards, 2000 L Street NW, Suite 411, Washington DC, 20036.

Meuller, Robert K.
Understanding Nonprofit Financial Statements: A Primer for Board Members. National Center for Nonprofit Boards, 2000 L Street NW, Suite 411, Washington DC, 20036.

O'Connell, Brian.
1985   *The Board Member Book.* Washington DC: The Foundation Center.

Park, Dabrey.
Strategic Planning and the Nonprofit Board. National Center for Nonprofit Boards, 2000 L Street NW, Suite 411, Washington DC, 20036.

Salamon, Lester M.
1992   *America's Nonprofit Sector: A Primer.* Baltimore, MD: Johns Hopkins University Press.

Senge, Peter M.
1990   *The Fifth Discipline.* New York: Doubleday.
A detailed projection for helping organizations to be "learning" organizations.

"Papers on Conciliation." Mennonite Central Committee, 21 South 12th Street, Akron, PA, 17501.

Strategic Planning for Nonprofits. Support Center of America, 2001 O Street NW, Washington DC, 20036-5955.

Index

INDEX

About the Authors

Edgar Stoesz has spent most of his adult life in nonprofit organizations, both as director and employee. A native Minnesotan, he held six different administrative posts with the Mennonite Central Committee, including seven years as Associate Executive Secretary. For 14 years he served as President–CEO of Mennonite Indemnity, a for profit reinsurance company serving mutual insurance companies.

He has served on the board of Habitat for Humanity, International since 1989, serving as chairman from 1991 to 1995. Additionally he has served on the board of Heifer Project, International, the American Leprosy Mission, Mennonite Economic Development Associates, Hospital Albert Schweitzer, and numerous other local and national boards.

In his administrative responsibilities, he has visited more than 50 countries. He has contributed articles to church papers and addressed audiences on a variety of subjects related to his service. Following a year of sabbatical leave at Cornell University in 1970 he wrote the book, *Beyond Good Intentions*.

Chester Raber, Ph.D., is a longtime organization and management consultant working with both for profit and not-for-profit organizations. He has focused on organization assessment and development, with particular attention to team-building, and management development, with particular attention to executive development.

He recently retired from Greenfield Associates, a private consulting firm which he founded and led from 1981-1992. Greenfield Associates was a subsidiary of High Industries, Inc., Lancaster Pennsylvania.

He has worked with many nonprofit boards, helping to establish, guide, and plan with them. His client list of boards includes hospitals, mental health organizations, retirement communities, colleges, communications enterprises, police, and others. He has paid special attention to the relationship between the chief executive officer and chairperson.

In other circumstances he has been chairman, officer, and member of numerous nonprofit boards.

Doing Good Better!
ORDER FORM

If you would like to order copies of *Doing Good Better!* for boards you know or are part of, use this form. (Discounts apply for more than one copy.)

Photocopy this page as often as you like.

The following discounts apply:

1 copy	$9.95
2-5 copies	$8.96 each (a 10% discount)
6-10 copies	$8.46 each (a 15% discount)
11-20 copies	$7.96 each (a 20% discount)

Prices subject to change.

Quantity   *Price*   *Total*

_____ copies of Doing Good Better! @ _____ _____

PA residents add 6% sales tax _____

Shipping & Handling
(add 10%, $3.00 minimum) _____

TOTAL _____

(Please fill in the payment and shipping information on the other side.)

METHOD OF PAYMENT

❐   Check or Money Order
     *(payable to **Good Books** in U.S. funds)*

❐   Please charge my:
     ❐ MasterCard   ❐ Visa   ❐ Discover   ❐ American Express

\# _____

exp. date _____

Signature _____

Name _____

Address_____

City _____

State _____

Zip_____

Phone _____

Email_____

SHIP TO: (if different)

Name _____

Address_____

City _____

State _____

Zip_____

Mail order to:
Good Books
P.O. Box 419 • Intercourse, PA 17534-0419
Call toll-free: 800/762-7171 • Fax number: 888/768-3433
www.goodbks.com
Prices subject to change.

Doing Good Better!
ORDER FORM

If you would like to order copies of *Doing Good Better!* for boards you know or are part of, use this form. (Discounts apply for more than one copy.)

Photocopy this page as often as you like.

The following discounts apply:

1 copy	$9.95
2-5 copies	$8.96 each (a 10% discount)
6-10 copies	$8.46 each (a 15% discount)
11-20 copies	$7.96 each (a 20% discount)

Prices subject to change.

Quantity   *Price*   *Total*

_____ copies of Doing Good Better! @ _____ _____

PA residents add 6% sales tax _____

Shipping & Handling
(add 10%, $3.00 minimum) _____

TOTAL _____

(Please fill in the payment and shipping information on the other side.)

METHOD OF PAYMENT

❒ Check or Money Order
    *(payable to **Good Books** in U.S. funds)*

❒ Please charge my:
    ❒ MasterCard   ❒ Visa   ❒ Discover   ❒ American Express

\# _____

exp. date _____

Signature _____

Name _____

Address_____

City _____

State _____

Zip_____

Phone _____

Email_____

SHIP TO: (if different)

Name _____

Address_____

City _____

State _____

Zip_____

Mail order to:
Good Books
P.O. Box 419 • Intercourse, PA 17534-0419
Call toll-free: 800/762-7171 • Fax number: 888/768-3433
www.goodbks.com
Prices subject to change.